Soups and Snacks

Kitchen Treasury Series

SOUPS and SNACKS

Editorial Director
DONALD D. WOLF

Design and Layout
MARGOT L. WOLF

Published by
LEXICON PUBLICATIONS, INC.
387 Park Avenue South, New York, NY 10016

Cover illustration:
Minestrone, 30

Opposite title page:
Tomato-Leek Soup, 73
Frankfurter Reuben, 74

Copyright © 1987 by
Advance Publishers
1146 Solana Avenue
Winter Park, Florida 32789

ISBN: 0-7172-4518-7

Contents

Soups

Gone is the soup of yesteryear—the heavy iron kettle that bubbled on the cook stove the livelong day. The fire-blackened pot has gone, but its legacy remains, and soup—thick or clear and all the varieties in between—is still a national favorite. Soup making is a fine test of a homemaker's skill in striking a harmonious balance of flavors. Much of the satisfaction and special pleasure of making soup come perhaps from the simple fact that nothing is more gratifying than good soup.

ENDLESS VARIETY—Soups, usually served as a first course, are main-dish fare too. Thin, clear soups (such as broths, bouillons and consommés), fruit soups, delicate cream soups, thick hearty soups (such as chowders and bisques), winter hot or summer cold—there is no end to variety.

REMINDERS—Always add hot, thickened tomatoes to cold milk to avoid curdling.

Thorough blending of fat and flour and cooking with the milk or cream help prevent a film of fat on cream soups. There will be a film of fat if soup is too thin. Cream soups should be the consistency of a thin sauce. The vegetable used will determine the amount of flour needed to thicken the soup. At least ¼ cup chopped or ⅓ cup sieved vegetable per cup of thin white sauce will give a most satisfactory soup; 2 to 3 tablespoons sieved spinach per cup is a desirable proportion for cream of spinach soup. Add a little hot milk or cream if the soup is too thick or thicken with a flour-water mixture if the soup is too thin.

Instructions for clarifying soups are given in Consommé (page 8).

The electric blender is the modern soup pot – blending everything and anything into savory soups. Remember – add liquid first, usually ½ to 1 cup, then add the other ingredients.

Cool soups to lukewarm before storing in covered container in refrigerator; keep several days only.

SOUP GARNISHES—Garnishes are to soup as jewels are to the costume—a glamorous accent. They need not be elaborate. The normally stocked refrigerator will usually yield the wherewithal for garnishes that furnish a touch of enticement.

Bacon—Diced and panbroiled, supplies a touch of crispness, color and flavor.

Croutons—Provide texture contrast (see page 35).

Grated Cheese—Parmesan is the classic accompaniment for onion soups, but other sharp cheeses enhance flavor of chowders and other soups.

Herbs—Chervil, chives, tarragon, parsley—fresh, minced or chopped—add a flash of color.

Lemon Slices—Notched or cut in fancy shapes and set afloat in clear bouillon or consommé.

Sour Cream—Connoisseur's preference for borsch.

Vegetables—Thin, small raw pieces floating on clear soups give appealing color and flavor.

Whipped Cream—Salted or plain; perfect with cream of tomato soup.

Toasted Almonds—Sliver; garnish cream soups.

STOCKS

Beef Stock

ABOUT
2½ QUARTS

3 pounds lean beef (chuck or plate), cut in 1-inch pieces
1 soup bone, cracked
3 quarts cold water
1½ tablespoons salt
2 large onions
2 whole cloves
5 carrots, pared and cut in large pieces
2 turnips, pared and cut in large pieces
3 stalks celery with leaves, sliced
4 leeks, sliced
Herb bouquet, (below)

1. Put meat and soup bone into a large saucepot; add water and salt. Cover and bring to boiling. Remove foam. Cover saucepot and simmer about 4 hours, removing foam as necessary.
2. Slice 1 onion; insert the cloves into second onion. Add onions, remaining vegetables, and herb bouquet to saucepot. Cover and bring to boiling. Reduce heat and simmer about 1½ hours.
3. Remove from heat; remove soup bone and strain stock through a fine sieve. Allow to cool. (The meat and vegetables strained from stock may be served as desired.)
4. Remove fat that rises to surface (reserve for use in other food preparation). Store stock in a covered container in refrigerator for future use, or reheat and serve with slices of crisp **toast.**

Brown Stock: Follow recipe for Beef Stock. Cut any meat from soup bone and brown the meat along with beef pices in **¼ cup fat** in saucepot before cooking. Proceed as in Beef Stock.

White Stock: Follow recipe for Beef Stock. Substitute **veal shank and breast** for beef. Add one half of a disjointed ready-to-cook **stewing chicken.**

Consommé: Follow recipe for White Stock. Cool stock and stir in **2 egg whites,** slightly beaten, **crushed shells of the eggs,** and **4 teaspoons water.** Heat slowly to boiling, stirring constantly. Remove from heat and let stand 25 minutes. Strain through two thicknesses of cheesecloth.

Bouillon: Follow recipe for Consommé. Substitute Brown Stock for White Stock.

Herb Bouquet: Tie neatly together **3 or 4 sprigs of parsley, 1 sprig thyme,** and **½ bay leaf.**

Meat Broth

ABOUT
1½ QUARTS

2 pounds beef shank or short ribs, or pork neckbones
1 pound marrow bones
3 quarts water
1 large onion, quartered
2 leaves cabbage
2 sprigs fresh parsley or 1 tablespoon dried parsley flakes
1 carrot, cut up
1 parsnip, cut up
1 stalk celery, cut up
5 peppercorns
1 tablespoon salt

1. Combine beef, bones, and water in a 6-quart kettle. Bring to boiling. Boil 15 minutes, skimming frequently.
2. Add remaining ingredients. Simmer rapidly about 1½ hours, or until meat is tender.
3. Strain off broth. Chill quickly. Skim off fat.
4. Remove meat from bones. Set meat aside for use in other dishes. Discard bones, vegetables, and peppercorns.
5. Return skimmed broth to kettle. Boil rapidly about 15 minutes, or until reduced to about 6 cups. Store in refrigerator until needed.

Meat Stock: Prepare Meat Broth as directed. Chill. Lift off fat. Boil until reduced to 3 cups, about 45 minutes.

Chicken Stock

3 TO 3½
QUARTS

5 pounds chicken backs and
  wings, or stewing chicken,
  cut up
3 carrots, cut in 2-inch
  pieces
2 medium yellow onions,
  quartered
1 stalk celery, cut in 2-inch
  pieces
2 teaspoons salt

Bouquet garni:
  ¾ teaspoon dried thyme
    leaves
  ¾ teaspoon dried rosemary
    leaves
  1 bay leaf
  4 sprigs parsley
  2 whole cloves
Water

1. Place chicken, vegetables, salt, and bouquet garni in an 8-quart Dutch oven. Pour in water to cover (about 4 quarts). Simmer covered 2 to 2½ hours.
2. Strain stock through a double thickness of cheesecloth into a storage container. Taste for seasoning. If more concentrated flavor is desired, return stock to saucepan and simmer 20 to 30 minutes, or dissolve 1 to 2 teaspoons instant chicken bouillon in the stock.
3. Store covered in refrigerator or freezer. Remove solidified fat from top of stock before using.

Note: Refrigerated stock is perishable. If not used within several days, heat to boiling, cool, and refrigerate or freeze to prevent spoilage. Stock can be kept frozen up to 4 months.

Fish Stock

ABOUT
1 QUART

2 pounds fresh lean fish with
  heads and bones, cut up
1 medium yellow onion,
  quartered
½ teaspoon salt
1 cup dry white wine
Water

Bouquet garni:
4 sprigs parsley
1 bay leaf
½ teaspoon dried thyme
  leaves
1 sprig celery leaves
2 peppercorns

1. Rinse fish under cold water. Place fish, onion, salt, wine, and bouquet garni in a 3-quart saucepan. Pour in water to cover (about 1½ quarts). Simmer covered 2 hours. Cool slightly.
2. Strain stock through a double thickness of cheesecloth into a storage container. Taste for seasoning. Add a small amount of salt and lemon juice, if desired. If a more concentrated flavor is desired, return stock to saucepan and simmer 30 to 45 minutes.
3. Store covered in refrigerator or freezer.

Note: Use white firm-fleshed fish such as halibut, cod, flounder, or lemon sole. Frozen fish can be used if necessary.
  Refrigerated stock is highly perishable. If not used within 2 days, heat to boiling, cool, and refrigerate or freeze to prevent spoilage. Stock can be kept frozen up to 2 months.

Brown Vegetable Stock

ABOUT
2 QUARTS

2 pounds mixed vegetables
  (carrots, leeks, onions,
  celery, turnips, etc.)
¼ cup butter or margarine
2½ quarts water
½ teaspoon salt
½ teaspoon thyme
3 sprigs parsley
½ bay leaf
Dash of pepper

1. Chop vegetables. Brown in butter.
2. Add water and seasonings. cover.
3. Simmer 1½ hours or until vegetables are tender.
4. Strain and chill.

White Vegetable Stock: If a lighter, clearer stock is desired, omit butter and do not brown vegetables.

LUNCH BOX SPECIALS

Tomato-Cheese Soup

3 SERVINGS

1 can (about 10 ounces)
  condensed tomato soup
1 soup can milk
1 cup (4 ounces) shredded
  Cheddar, American, or
  Colby cheese
¼ teaspoon finely crushed
  basil (optional)

1. Turn soup into a large saucepan; gradually blend in milk. Stir until hot and blended.
2. Mix in cheese and, if desired, basil.

Suggested accompaniment: Pocket Bread with desired filling (below).

Pocket Bread

20 POCKET
BREADS

2 cups all-purpose flour
2 packages active dry yeast
2 tablespoons sugar or
  honey
2 teaspoons salt
2½ cups hot water
  (120°-130°F)
¼ cup vegetable oil
5½ to 6 cups all-purpose
  flour

1. Combine 2 cups flour, yeast, sugar, and salt in a large mixing bowl.
2. Stir in water and oil; beat until smooth.
3. Stir in enough remaining flour to make a soft dough.
4. Turn onto a floured surface; continue to work in flour until stiff enough to knead. Knead until smooth and elastic (about 5 minutes).
5. Place in an oiled bowl; turn to oil top of dough. Cover; let rise in a warm place until double in bulk (about 45 minutes).
6. Punch dough down. Divide in half. Divide each half into 10 equal pieces. Roll each piece into a ball. Let dough rest 5 minutes. Roll balls into 3- or 4-inch rounds, ⅛ inch thick. Place on greased baking sheets. Cover; let rise 30 minutes (see Note).
7. Bake at 450°F 5 to 8 minutes, or until puffed and brown.

Note: Avoid pinching or creasing dough after rolling, or bread will not puff properly.

Hot Dog! It's Soup

6 TO 8
SERVINGS

½ cup chopped onion
⅓ cup sliced celery
2 tablespoons margarine
1 cup water
2 cups (16-ounce can)
  cream-style corn
1 bay leaf
½ teaspoon basil
1½ cups milk
1 pound frankfurters, sliced
1 teaspoon salt
⅛ teaspoon pepper
½ cup shredded process
  American cheese
Minced parsley

1. Sauté onion and celery in margarine in a medium saucepan. Add water, corn, bay leaf, and basil. Cook 5 minutes.
2. Remove bay leaf. Add remaining ingredients except parsley. Cook over low heat until cheese melts.
3. Garnish with parsley.

Alphabet Soup

6 TO 8
SERVINGS

½ pound ground beef
1 onion, chopped
5 cups water
1 can (16 ounces) tomatoes
3 potatoes, cubed
2 carrots, sliced
2 stalks celery, sliced
2 teaspoons salt
1 teaspoon Worcestershire
   sauce
1 beef bouillon cube
¼ teaspoon garlic powder
¼ teaspoon pepper
3 sprigs fresh parsley,
   minced, or 2
   tablespoons dried
1 cup uncooked alphabet
   macaroni

1. Brown meat in a large saucepan; drain off fat.
2. Add remaining ingredients, except macaroni. Bring to boiling; cover and simmer 1 hour.
3. Stir in macaroni; cook 20 minutes.

Suggested accompaniment: banana bread-cream cheese sandwiches (see Grandma Louise's Banana Loaf below).

Grandma's Louise's Banana Loaf

1 LOAF

1 cup sugar
½ cup shortening
1 cup mashed fully ripe
   bananas (2 to 3
   bananas)
1 egg
¼ cup buttermilk
1¾ cups all-purpose flour
1½ teaspoons baking powder
1 teaspoon baking soda
½ teaspoon salt

1. Combine sugar, shortening, bananas, egg, and buttermilk in a mixing bowl; beat well.
2. Blend remaining ingedients, add to banana mixture, and mix until blended (about 1 minute).
3. Turn into a greased 9 x 5 x 3-inch loaf pan.
4. Bake at 350°F 45 to 50 minutes, or until done.

Bean and Prosciutto Soup

10 TO 12
SERVINGS

2 cups (about ¾ pound)
   dried beans, soaked
   overnight
5 cups water
2 cups sliced celery
3 to 4 ounces sliced
   prosciutto, cut in thin
   strips
1 can (16 ounces) tomatoes
1 can (about 10 ounces)
   condensed beef broth
1 teaspoon salt
1 garlic clove, crushed
2 packages (9 ounces each)
   frozen Italian green
   beans
3 sprigs fresh parsley,
   minced (about 2
   tablespoons)

1. Combine soaked dried beans, water, celery, prosciutto, tomatoes, beef broth, salt, and garlic in a 5-quart saucepot. Bring to boiling; simmer, covered, 30 minutes.
2. Mix in green beans and parsley; simmer 5 to 10 minutes.

Biscuits and New England Blueberry Muffins

Homemade Chicken-Noodle Soup

8 SERVINGS

2 quarts water
1 broiler-fryer chicken
   (about 2½ pounds), cut
   up
1 finely chopped onion
1 finely chopped celery
2 tablespoons minced fresh
   parsley or 1 teaspoon
   dried
2 teaspoons salt
1 teaspoon crushed
   rosemary or chervil
⅛ teaspoon pepper
2 cups uncooked homemade
   (see below) or
   packaged noodles

1. Place all ingredients except noodles in a kettle or Dutch oven. Bring to boiling; simmer 1 hour, or until chicken is tender.
2. Remove chicken; cool. Discard skin. Remove meat from bones and chop.
3. Return chicken to stock; bring to boiling. Stir in noodles. Simmer 20 to 30 minutes, or until noodles are done.

Suggested accompaniment: New England Blueberry Muffins (below).

Homemade Noodles

2 CUPS
NOODLES

2 eggs
½ teaspoon salt
1 cup all-purpose flour

1. Beat eggs and salt in a mixing bowl. Gradually add flour, mixing well until mixture forms a soft dough. Turn onto a flour surface; knead in remaining flour to form a very stiff dough.
2. Cover; let rest 10 to 15 minutes.
3. Roll dough as thin as possible, turning dough over as you roll.
4. Roll dough up tightly, jelly-roll fashion. Cut off thin slices. Toss to separate. Spread out on baking sheets; toss periodically until thoroughly dry.

New England Blueberry Muffins

12 LARGE
MUFFINS

1 cup sugar
½ cup softened butter or
   margarine
2 eggs
½ cup milk
2 cups all-purpose flour
2 teaspoons baking powder
½ teaspoon salt
1 to 1½ fresh or frozen
   blueberries

1. Combine sugar, butter, eggs, and milk in a mixing bowl; beat well.
2. Blend flour, baking powder, and salt; add and mix until blended (about 1 minute). Fold in blueberries.
3. Spoon into 12 well-greased muffin cups, filling almost to the top of the cup.
4. Bake at 375°F 20 to 25 minutes.

MAIN DISH SOUPS

Soup Kettle Supper

ABOUT
8 SERVINGS

¼ pound sliced bacon, cut in
  pieces
2 cups diced cooked ham
1 can (10½ ounces)
  condensed beef broth
2 cups water
1⅓ cups packaged pre-
  cooked rice
1 can (17 ounces) whole
  kernel corn
1 can (16 ounces) green
  beans
1 can (16 ounces) tomatoes
1 to 2 teaspoons salt
⅛ teaspoon pepper
1 tablespoon finely chopped
  parsley

1. Fry bacon in a kettle or Dutch oven until crisp. Remove bacon and drain on absorbent paper.
2. Pour off all but 2 tablespoons of the drippings. Fry ham in the hot bacon drippings in kettle until slightly browned.
3. Add bacon and remaining ingredients except parsley. Bring to boiling; cover and remove from heat; let stand 5 minutes.
4. Sprinkle rice mixture with parsley and serve.

Beef Soup

6 SERVINGS

1½ pounds beef for stew
1 soup bone
1½ to 2 teaspoons salt
½ teaspoon pepper
2 bay leaves
4 medium-sized carrots,
  pared and sliced
1 cup chopped cabbage
1 cup chopped celery
½ cup chopped onion
1 can (15 ounces) Italian-
  style tomatoes
1 tablespoon Worcestershire
  sauce
1 beef fouillon cube
Pinch oregano (or other herb
  desired)

1. Put meat and soup bone in a heavy 3-quart kettle; cover with cold water (about 4 cups). Add salt, pepper, and bay leaves. Bring rapidly to boiling. Reduce heat. Add carrots, cabbage, celery, and onion; cover and simmer until meat is tender, about 2½ hours.
2. Remove and discard bone and bay leaves. Cut meat into bite-size pieces and return to soup. Mix in tomatoes, Worcestershire sauce, bouillon cube, and oregano. Cover and simmer 30 minutes.

Beef Barley Soup

8 TO 10
SERVINGS

2 quarts water
1 soup bone with meat
½ cup chopped celery tops
1 tablespoon salt
½ teaspoon pepper
½ cup uncooked regular
  barley
3 cups coarsely chopped
  cabbage
1 cup sliced carrots
1 cup sliced celery
2 cups sliced parsnips
2 cups thinly sliced onion
1 can (12 ounces) tomato
  paste

1. Combine water, bone, celery tops, salt, and pepper in a Dutch oven. Bring to boiling; cover tightly and simmer 1 to 2 hours.
2. Remove bone from stock; cool. Remove meat from bone; chop. Return to stock.
3. Stir in barley; continue cooking 30 minutes.
4. Add remaining ingredients; simmer 30 minutes, or until vegetables are tender.

Beef Barley Soup

Caraway-Cabbage Soup

12 CUPS;
8 TO 12
SERVINGS

3 tablespoons butter or
  margarine
1 head (2 pounds) cabbage,
  coarsely chopped
5 cups chicken stock
1 teaspoon caraway seed
¼ teaspoon pepper
1 can or bottle (12 ounces)
  beer
⅓ cup flour
1 cup cream, half-and-half,
  or milk
Salt

Caraway-Cabbage Soup

1. Melt butter; add cabbage. Cook slowly, stirring often,
until limp.
2. Add stock, caraway seed, and pepper. Cover and simmer about 1 hour, adding beer during last 10 minutes.
3. Mix flour and a little cream to a smooth paste; add remaining cream. Stir into soup. Cook, stirring constantly, until
bubbly and slightly thickened. Season to taste with salt.

Chinese Cabbage Soup

6 SERVINGS

2 cups cooked chicken, cut
  into strips (about 1 chicken
  breast)
7 cups chicken broth
6 cups sliced Chinese cabbage (celery cabbage)
1 teaspoon soy sauce
1 teaspoon salt
¼ teaspoon pepper

Combine chicken and chicken broth; bring to boiling. Stir
in remaining ingredients; cook only 3 to 4 minutes, or just
until cabbage is crisp-tender. (Do not overcook.)

Note: If desired, lettuce may be substituted for the Chinese
cabbage. Reduce cooking time to 1 minute.

Dill Cabbage Soup

8 TO 10
SERVINGS

2 quarts beef stock
1 cup thinly sliced carrots
1 cup sliced celery
½ cup chopped onion
8 cups (about ½ head) thinly
  sliced cabbage
Salt and pepper to taste
3 tablespoons water
2 tablespoons flour
½ cup yogurt or dairy sour
  half-and-half
½ teaspoon minced dill or ¼
  teaspoon dried dill weed
Minced parsley

1. Pour stock into a large saucepan. Add carrots, celery,
and onion. Bring to boiling, reduce heat, and cook until
vegetables are tender (about 10 minutes).
2. Add cabbage; continue cooking until crisp-tender (about
5 minutes). Season to taste with salt and pepper.
3. Stir water gradually into flour, stirring until smooth. Pour
slowly into soup, stirring constantly. Bring to boiling; boil
1 minute.
4. Stir in yogurt and dill.
5. Garnish with parsley.

Pumpkin Patch Soup

4 SERVINGS

3 cups canned pumpkin or fresh cooked puréed pumpkin
2 cups milk, half-and-half, or 1 can (13 ounces) evaporated milk
3 tablespoons maple syrup
1 teaspoon salt
½ teaspoon nutmeg
½ teaspoon cinnamon
¼ teaspoon cloves or allspice

Combine all ingredients in a large saucepan. Heat.

Baked Minestrone

10 TO 12 SERVINGS

1½ pounds lean beef for stew, cut in 1-inch cubes
1 cup coarsely chopped onion
2 cloves garlic, crushed
1 teaspoon salt
¼ teaspoon pepper
2 tablespoons olive oil
3 cans (about 10 ounces each) condensed beef broth
2 soup cans water
1½ teaspoons herb seasoning
1 can (16 ounces) tomatoes (undrained)
1 can (15¼ ounces) kidney beans (undrained)
1½ cups thinly sliced carrots
1 cup small seashell macaroni
2 cups sliced zucchini
Grated Parmesan cheese

1. Mix beef, onion, garlic, salt, and pepper in a large saucepan. Add olive oil and stir to coat meat evenly.
2. Bake at 400°F 30 minutes, or until meat is browned, stirring occasionally.
3. Turn oven control to 350°F. Add broth, water, and seasonings; stir. Cover; cook 1 hour, or until meat is tender.
4. Stir in tomatoes, kidney beans, olives, carrots, and macaroni. Put sliced zucchini on top. Cover; bake 30 to 40 minutes, or until carrots are tender.
5. Serve with grated cheese.

Baked Minestrone

Meatball Soup

8 SERVINGS

1 pound ground beef
1 onion, chopped
1½ quarts water
1 can (16 ounces) tomatoes
3 potatoes, cubed
2 carrots, sliced
2 stalks celery, sliced
3 sprigs fresh parsley,
  minced, or 2 tablespoons
  dried
½ cup uncooked barley
2 teaspoons salt
½ teaspoon crushed thyme
  or basil
¼ teaspoon garlic powder
¼ teaspoon pepper
1 bay leaf
1 teaspoon Worcestershire
  sauce
1 beef bouillon cube

1. Shape beef into tiny meatballs. Brown meatballs and onion in a large saucepan, or place in a shallow pan and brown in a 400°F oven. Drain off excess fat.
2. Add remaining ingredients. Bring to boiling, simmer 1½ hours, or until vegetables are tender.

Pioneer Potato Soup

4 TO 6 SERVINGS

1 quart chicken stock
4 potatoes, chopped (about 4
  cups)
2 cups sliced carrots
½ cup sliced celery
¼ cup chopped onion
1 teaspoon salt
½ teaspoon marjoram, dill
  weed, or cumin
⅛ teaspoon white pepper
1 cup milk or half-and-half
2 tablespoons flour
Garnishes: paprika, sliced
  green onions, crisply
  cooked crumbled bacon,
  chopped pimento, snipped
  chives or parsley, or grated
  Parmesan cheese

1. Combine all ingredients except milk, flour, and garnishes in a large saucepan. Bring to boiling; simmer 30 minutes.
2. Gradually add milk to flour, stirring until smooth. Stir into soup.
3. Bring soup to boiling; boil 1 minute, stirring constantly.
4. Garnish as desired.

Potato Soup with Sour Cream: Follow recipe for Pioneer Potato Soup. Before serving, stir in ½ **cup sour cream.** Heat; do not boil.

Puréed Potato Soup: Follow recipe for either Pioneer Potato or Potato Soup with Sour Cream, omitting the flour. Purée in an electric blender before serving. Reheat, if necessary.

Chili Soup

8 TO 10 SERVINGS

½ pound ground beef
1 cup chopped onion
5 cups water
1 can (28 ounces) tomatoes
1 can (15 ounces) tomato
  sauce
1 clove garlic, crushed
1 tablespoon chili powder
1 teaspoon salt
1 teaspoon cumin
½ teaspoon oregano
1 cup uncooked macaroni
1 can (about 15 ounces)
  kidney or chili beans

1. Brown meat in a large saucepan; drain off fat. Stir in onion; cook 1 minute.
2. Add water, tomatoes, tomato sauce, garlic, chili powder, salt, cumin, and oregano. Simmer 30 minutes.
3. Add remaining ingredients; cook until macaroni is done (about 10 to 15 minutes).

Chili-Chicken Soup

6 TO 8
SERVINGS

1 broiler-fryer chicken (about 3 pounds), cut up
1½ quarts water
1 onion, studded with 2 or 3 whole cloves
1 tablespoon salt
3 garlic cloves, crushed
1 bay leaf
1 can (about 15 ounces) red kidney beans
1 can (6 ounces) tomato paste
1 can (4 ounces) mild green chilies or 1 hot pepper, chopped
1 tablespoon chili powder
1 teaspoon crushed basil
Cooked rice

1. Combine chicken, water, onion, salt, garlic, and bay leaf in a large saucepan. Bring to boiling; simmer 45 minutes, or until chicken is tender.
2. Remove chicken and onion from stock; cool. Discard chicken skin; remove meat from bones and chop. Skim fat from stock (see page 8). Remove cloves from onion; discard. Chop onion.
3. Stir chicken, onion, and remaining ingredients, except rice, into stock. Heat. Serve with rice.

Chicken Succotash Soup with Parsley Dumplings

6 TO 8
SERVINGS

1 broiler-fryer chicken (2 to 3 pounds), cut up
2 quarts water
2 teaspoons salt
½ teaspoon crushed rosemary
Pinch pepper
Parsley Dumplings (below)
1 cup sliced carrots
¼ cup chopped onion
1 package (10 ounces) frozen corn
1 package (10 ounces) frozen lima beans

1. Combine chicken, water, salt, rosemary, and pepper in a large saucepan. Bring to boiling; simmer 45 minutes, covered, or until chicken is tender.
2. Remove chicken from broth; cool, skin, and cut into pieces.
3. Skim fat or chill to remove fat (see page 8).
4. Prepare Parsley Dumplings.
5. Add vegetables and chicken to stock. Bring to boiling. Drop dumplings by teaspoonfuls onto gently simmering soup. Cover; cook 10 minutes. Uncover; cook 5 to 10 minutes.
6. Serve each portion with one or two dumplings.

Parsley Dumplings

2 cups all-purpose flour
2 teaspoons baking powder
1½ teaspoons salt
⅛ teaspoon pepper
3 tablespoons butter or margarine
1 egg
Milk
¼ cup minced parsley

1. Combine flour, baking powder, salt, and pepper in a bowl.
2. Cut in butter until mixture resembles coarse meal.
3. Break egg into measuring cup. Add enough milk to make 1 cup liquid. Beat well. Add to dry ingredients along with parsley and stir just until flour is moistened.
4. Proceed as directed.

Cream of Broccoli Soup

6 SERVINGS

2 packages (10 ounces each) frozen chopped broccoli
1 cup water
½ cup sliced celery
1 small onion, sliced
2 tablespoons butter or margarine
2 tablespoons flour
1½ quarts chicken stock
2 egg yolks, beaten
½ cup half-and-half or milk
½ teaspoon salt
Pinch pepper
Paprika

1. Cook broccoli in water 3 to 5 minutes; reserve liquid.
2. Sauté celery and onion in butter; stir in flour. Gradually add stock and liquid from broccoli, stirring constantly, until thickened.
3. Add broccoli; put through a food mill or purée in an electric blender, if desired.
4. Stir egg yolks into half-and-half; gradually add to soup, being careful not to boil. Season with salt and pepper.
5. Garnish each serving with a sprinkle of paprika.

Creamy Cheddar Cheese Soup

ABOUT 2 QUARTS

2 tablespoons butter
2 tablespoons chopped onion
⅓ cup all-purpose flour
1¼ teaspoons dry mustard
¼ teaspoon garlic powder
¼ teaspoon paprika
2 teaspoons Worcestershire sauce
1½ quarts milk
3 tablespoons chicken seasoned stock base
1½ cups sliced celery
2½ cups (10 ounces) shredded Cheddar cheese

1. Melt butter in a 3-quart saucepan. Add onion and sauté until tender. Stir in flour, mustard, garlic powder, paprika, and Worcestershire sauce.
2. Remove from heat; gradually add milk, stirring constantly. Add chicken stock base and celery; mix well. Cook over low heat, stirring occasionally, until thickened. Add cheese and stir until cheese is melted and soup is desired serving temperature; do not boil.
3. Serve topped with **chopped green pepper, pimento strips, toasted slivered almonds,** or **cooked crumbled bacon.**

Brussels Sprout Soup

ABOUT 20 SERVINGS

4 packages (10 ounces each) frozen Brussels sprouts
7 bouillon cubes
5 cups boiling water
8 slices bacon, diced
2 cloves garlic, minced
6 cups milk
¾ cup uncooked rice
1 teaspoon oregano leaves, crushed
2 teaspoons salt
½ teaspoon pepper
1 package (10 ounces) frozen peas and carrots
1 teaspoon salt
2 cups water
¾ cup shredded Parmesan cheese
Assorted crackers

1. Set out a large saucepot or Dutch oven and a saucepan.
2. Partially thaw frozen Brussels sprouts.
3. Make chicken broth by dissolving bouillon cubes in boiling water. Set aside.
4. Fry in saucepot or Dutch oven the bacon and garlic.
5. Add 3 cups of the broth to saucepot with milk, uncooked rice, and a mixture of oregano leaves, salt and pepper.
6. Bring to boiling, reduce heat and simmer covered 15 minutes.
7. Add to saucepot the frozen peas and carrots. Bring to boiling, reduce heat and simmer about 10 minutes, or until vegetables are tender.
8. Meanwhile, coarsely chop the partially thawed Brussels sprouts. Combine in saucepan the remaining 2 cups of broth, salt and 2 cups water.
9. Bring to boiling and add the chopped Brussels sprouts. Return to boiling and simmer uncovered 10 minutes, or until tender.
10. Add Brussels sprouts with their cooking liquid to rice mixture. Stir in shredded Parmesan cheese. Accompany with assorted crackers.

Brussels Sprout Soup

Cream of Turkey Soup

ABOUT
6 SERVINGS

½ cup butter
6 tablespoons flour
½ teaspoon salt
Pinch black pepper
2 cups half-and-half
3 cups turkey or chicken
broth
¾ cup coarsely chopped
cooked turkey

1. Heat butter in a saucepan. Blend in flour, salt, and pepper. Heat until bubbly.
2. Gradually add half-and-half and 1 cup of broth, stirring constantly. Bring to boiling; cook and stir 1 to 2 minutes.
3. Blend in remaining broth and turkey. Heat; do not boil. Garnish with grated carrot.

Frankfurter-Chicken Cream Soup

ABOUT
6 SERVINGS

2 tablespoons butter
1 medium-sized onion, cut in
¼-inch slices
5 frankfurters, cut in ¼-inch
slices
1 can (10 ounces) condensed
cream of chicken soup
1 soup can water
1 soup can milk
2 chicken bouillon cubes
¼ teaspoon ground mace
½ teaspoon grated lemon
peel

1. Heat butter in a saucepan. Add onion and frankfurter slices. Cook until onion is transparent, occasionally moving and turning with a spoon.
2. Stir in the soup, then the water and milk, blending thoroughly after each addition.
3. Add bouillon cubes, stirring occasionally until completely dissolved. Stir in the mace and lemon peel and heat thoroughly (do not boil). Garnish with **minced parsley**

Carrot-Pea Cream Soup

4 TO 6
SERVINGS

1 can (10½ ounces)
condensed cream of
chicken soup
1 can (11¼ ounces) condensed green pea soup-
1½ cups milk
1 cup heavy cream
½ cup cooked sliced carrots
½ teaspoon grated onion
¼ teaspoon freshly ground
black pepper
¼ teaspoon ground thyme

1. Blend the soups and gradually add the milk and cream, stirring until well blended.
2. Add the remaining ingredients and cook over medium heat, stirring occasionally, until thoroughly heated.

Lettuce Soup

ABOUT
3 SERVINGS

2 tablespoons butter or
margarine
2 tablespoons flour
1 can (about 10 ounces) condensed chicken broth
1 soup can water
½ small head lettuce, cored
and coarsely chopped
¼ cup thinly sliced celery
1 tablespoon chopped
watercress
Salt and pepper

1. Melt butter in a saucepot; stir in flour and cook until bubbly.
2. Gradually stir in chicken broth and water; bring to boiling, stirring constantly. Cook 1 minute.
3. Stir in lettuce, celery, and watercress. Season with salt and pepper to taste. Cook until vegetables are crisp-tender, about 5 minutes.

Lettuce Soup

Farm-Style Leek Soup

6 SERVINGS,
ABOUT
1½ CUPS EACH

2 large leeks (1 pound) with part of green tops, sliced
2 medium onions, sliced
1 large garlic clove, minced
¼ cup butter or margarine
4 cups chicken stock or bouillon
2 cups uncooked narrow or medium noodles (3 ounces)
1 can or bottle (12 ounces) beer
1½ cups shredded semisoft cheese (Muenster, brick, process, etc.)
Salt and pepper

1. Cook leek, onion, and garlic in butter for 15 minutes, using low heat and stirring often.
2. Add stock. Cover and simmer 30 minutes.
3. Add noodles. Cover and simmer 15 minutes, or until noodles are tender.
4. Add beer; heat to simmering. Gradually add cheese, cooking slowly and stirring until melted. Season to taste with salt and pepper.

Sweet Pea Soup

6 SERVINGS

1 small head lettuce, shredded (about 5 cups)
2 cups shelled fresh peas, or 1 package (10 ounces) frozen green peas
1 cup water
½ cup chopped leek or green onion
2 tablespoons butter
2 teaspoons chervil
1 teaspoon sugar
½ teaspoon salt
¼ teaspoon black pepper
1 can (about 10 ounces) condensed beef broth
¾ cup water
2 cups half-and-half

1. Put lettuce, peas, 1 cup water, leek, butter, chervil, sugar, salt, and pepper into a large saucepan; stir and bring to boiling. Cover and cook until peas are tender.
2. Press mixture through a coarse sieve or food mill and return to saucepan. Stir in broth and ¾ cup water.
3. Just before serving, stir half-and-half into mixture and heat.

Split Pea-Vegetable Soup

ABOUT 2½ QUARTS SOUP

1¼ cups dried green split peas, rinsed
1 quart water
2 leeks, washed thoroughly and cut in large pieces
1 large onion, peeled and cut in large pieces
4 green onions, diced
2 carrots, pared and diced
2 tablespoons butter
¼ pound fresh mushrooms, cleaned and diced
1 cup defrosted frozen cut okra
1 cup defrosted frozen whole kernel corn
1 teaspoon salt
Few grains pepper
1 can (about 13 ounces) chicken broth

1. Put split peas into an electric cooker. Add water, cover, and let stand overnight.
2. The next day, add leek, onion, and carrot to cooker; mix.
3. Cover and cook on High 5 hours.
4. Heat butter in a skillet. Add mushrooms and cook until lightly browned.
5. Add browned mushrooms, okra, corn, salt, pepper, and broth to vegetable mixture; stir.
6. Cover and cook on High 1 hour.
7. Serve garnished with **sour cream** and **snipped parsley.**

Split Pea Soup

6 TO 8 SERVINGS

1 pound dried split peas, rinsed
1½ pounds smoked ham hocks
1 cup chopped onion
½ cup sliced celery
2 teaspoons salt
6 whole peppercorns
1 bay leaf
1½ quarts water

1. Put all ingredients into an electric cooker.
2. Cover and cook on Low 8 to 10 hours.
3. Remove ham hocks and dice meat; reserve ham. Discard bay leaf and peppercorns.
4. Pour soup, about one quarter at a time, into an electric blender and blend until smooth. Return soup to cooker, mix in ham, and keep hot until serving time.

Yellow Pea Soup with Pork

ABOUT
2½ QUARTS

¾ pound (about 1⅔ cups)
  yellow peas
2½ quarts cold water
1 1-pound piece smoked
  shoulder roll
3 quarts water
¾ cup coarsely chopped
  onion
1 teaspoon salt
1 teaspoon whole thyme
¼ teaspoon sugar

1. Rinse, sort (discarding imperfect peas) and put peas into a large saucepan.
2. Pour 2½ quarts cold water over the peas.
3. Cover and set peas aside to soak overnight.
4. The next day, set out shoulder roll.
5. Put the shoulder roll, water and onion into a large sauce pot.
6. Simmer 1½ to 2 hours, or until meat is tender.
7. Remove meat and set aside. Skim off fat from liquid, leaving about 2 tablespoons. Drain the peas and add to the broth with salt, whole thyme, and sugar.
8. Simmer 1½ to 2 hours, or until peas are tender. If necessary, skim off shells of peas as they come to the surface.
9. Serve soup with thin slices of the meat.

Vegetable Medley Soup

ABOUT
6 SERVINGS

8 slices bacon
½ cup chopped onion
½ cup sliced celery
5 cups water
1½ cups fresh corn or 1
  package (about 10 ounces)
  frozen corn
½ cup sliced carrots
1 potato, pared and sliced
1 tablespoon salt
1 teaspoon sugar
¼ teaspoon crushed thyme or
  basil
1 cup fresh green beans, cut in
  1-inch pieces
4 cups chopped peeled tomatoes
  (4 to 5 tomatoes)

1. Cook bacon until crisp in a Dutch oven or kettle. Drain off all but 2 tablespoons fat.
2. Sauté onion and celery in bacon fat.
3. Stir in water, corn, carrots, potato, salt, sugar, pepper, and thyme, Bring to boiling; simmer covered 30 minutes.
4. Stir in green beans; simmer 10 minutes, or until beans are crisp-tender.
5. Stir in tomatoes; heat 5 minutes.

Bean Soup

6 TO 8
SERVINGS

1 cup large dried white
  beans
2 quarts water
1 cup sliced celery (½-inch
  pieces)
2 cups chopped onion
4 medium carrots, cut in
  ½-inch slices
½ cup chopped parsley
1 tablespoon tomato paste
1 cup olive oil
1 tablespoon oregano,
  crushed
3 tablespoons wine vinegar

1. Bring beans to a boil in the water. Reduce heat and simmer 1 hour.
2. Add remaining ingredients. Simmer 2 hours more.
3. Add **salt** and **pepper** to taste. Serve with **toasted bread.**

Vegetable Medley Soup

Ham-Bean Soup

ABOUT
4 QUARTS
SOUP

2 quarts water
1 pound (about 2 cups) dried
  Great Northern or pea
  beans
3 tablespoons butter
2 cups finely chopped onion
½ cup finely chopped celery
2 teaspoons finely chopped
  garlic
3 cans (about 10 ounces
  each) condensed chicken broth
Water
1 ham shank (about 4
  pounds) or 2 ham hocks
  (about 1½ pounds)
1 can (about 16 ounces)
  tomatoes or 4 to 6 medium-
  sized firm ripe tomatoes,
  peeled and chopped
2 whole cloves
1 bay leaf
¼ teaspoon freshly ground
  black pepper
2 cups shredded Cheddar
  cheese (about 8 ounces)

1. Bring water to boiling in a 6-quart saucepot. Add beans gradually to water so that boiling continues. Boil 2 minutes. Remove from heat and set aside 1 hour.

2. Drain beans, reserving liquid. Return beans to saucepot along with 4 cups of cooking liquid.

3. Melt butter in a large skillet. Add onion, celery, and garlic; cook 5 minutes, stirring occasionally. Turn contents of skillet into saucepot.

4. Combine chicken broth with enough water to make 6 cups. Pour into saucepot.

5. Peel skin from ham shank and cut off excess fat. Add shank and skin to saucepot along with tomatoes, cloves, bay leaf, and pepper. Bring to boiling, reduce heat, and simmer 2 to 2½ hours, or until ham is tender.

6. Remove ham shank and skin; cool. Transfer soup to a large bowl; remove bay leaf and cloves. Cut meat into pieces and return to soup. Refrigerate, then skim off fat.

7. Transfer soup to saucepot and bring to simmer. Add cheese and stir until melted.

Note: Soup may be stored in the refrigerator and reheated, or cooled and poured into freezer containers and frozen. Thaw and reheat over low heat.

Black Bean Soup

ABOUT
2 QUARTS
SOUP

1 pound dried black beans,
  washed
2 quarts boiling water
2 tablespoons salt
5 cloves garlic
1½ teaspoons cumin
  (comino)
1½ teaspoons oregano
2 tablespoons white vinegar
10 tablespoons olive oil
½ pound onions, peeled and
  chopped
½ pound green peppers,
  trimmed and chopped

1. Put beans into a large, heavy saucepot or Dutch oven and add boiling water; boil rapidly 2 minutes. Cover tightly, remove from heat, and set aside 1 hour. Add salt to beans and liquid; bring to boiling and simmer, covered, until beans are soft, about 2 hours.

2. Put the garlic, cumin, oregano, and vinegar into a mortar and crush to a paste.

3. Heat olive oil in a large skillet. Mix in onion and green pepper and fry until onion is browned, stirring occasionally. Thoroughly blend in the paste, then stir in the skillet mixture into the beans. Cook over low heat until ready to serve.

4. Meanwhile, mix a small portion of **cooked rice, minced onion, olive oil,** and **vinegar** in a bowl; set aside to marinate. Add a soup spoon of rice mixture to each serving of soup.

Lentil Soup

6 TO 8
SERVINGS

1 package (16 ounces) dried
  lentils
2 quarts water
½ cup olive oil
1 cup chopped celery
½ cup grated carrot
1 onion, quartered
1 tablespoon tomato paste
3 garlic cloves, peeled
2 bay leaves
Salt and pepper to taste
Vinegar

1. Rinse lentils several times. Drain.

2. In a kettle put lentils, water, olive oil, celery, carrot, onion, tomato paste, garlic, bay leaves, salt, and pepper. Bring to a boil. Reduce heat and simmer covered 2 hours. Adjust salt and pepper.

3. Serve with a cruet of vinegar.

Ham-Bean Soup

SOUPS FROM AROUND THE WORLD

Minestrone from Italy

ABOUT
6 SERVINGS

6 cups water
1¼ cups (about ½ pound)
dried navy beans, rinsed
¼ pound salt pork
3 tablespoons olive oil
1 small onion, chopped
1 clove garlic, chopped
¼ head cabbage
2 stalks celery, cut in ½-inch
slices
2 small carrots, pared and
cut in ½-inch slices
1 medium potato, pared and
diced
1 tablespoon chopped parsley
½ teaspoon salt
¼ teaspoon pepper
1 quart hot water
¼ cup packaged precooked
rice
½ cup frozen green peas
¼ cup tomato paste
Grated Parmesan cheese

1. Bring the 6 cups water to boiling in a large saucepot. Gradually add the beans to the boiling water so the boiling does not stop. Simmer the beans 2 minutes, and remove from heat. Set aside to soak 1 hour.
2. Add salt pork to beans and return to heat. Bring to boiling, reduce heat, and simmer 1 hour, stirring once or twice.
3. While beans are simmering with salt pork, heat the olive oil in a skillet, and brown the onion and garlic lightly. Set aside.
4. Wash the cabbage, discarding coarse outer leaves, and shred finely.
5. After the beans have simmered an hour, add the onion, garlic, celery, carrots, potato, cabbage, parsley, salt, and pepper. Slowly pour in 1 quart hot water and simmer about 1 hour, or until the beans are tender.
6. Meanwhile, cook the rice according to package directions. About 10 minutes before the beans should be done, stir in the rice and peas. When the peas are tender, stir in the tomato paste. Simmer about 5 minutes. Serve sprinkled with cheese.

Vegetable Soup Italienne

ABOUT
6 SERVINGS

2 tablespoons butter
2 tablespoons cooking or
salad oil
1 cup thinly sliced carrots
1 cup thinly sliced zucchini
1 cup thinly sliced celery
1 cup finely shredded
cabbage
2 beef bouillon cubes
8 cups boiling water
2 teaspoons salt
2 medium-sized tomatoes,
cut in pieces
½ cup uncooked broken
spaghetti
½ teaspoon thyme

1. Heat the butter and oil in a saucepot. Add the carrots, zucchini, celery, and cabbage. Cook, uncovered, about 10 minutes, stirring occasionally.
2. Add the bouillon cubes, water, and salt. Bring to boiling; reduce heat and simmer, uncovered, 30 minutes.
3. Stir in tomatoes, spaghetti, and thyme; cook 20 minutes longer.
4. Serve hot from a tureen with **shredded Parmesan cheese** sprinkled over the top of each serving.

Roman Egg Soup with Noodles

4 SERVINGS

4 cups chicken broth
1½ tablespoons semolina or
flour
1½ tablespoons grated
Parmesan cheese
⅛ teaspoon salt
⅛ teaspoon pepper
4 eggs, well beaten
1 cup cooked noodles
Snipped parsley

1. Bring chicken broth to boiling.
2. Meanwhile, mix semolina, cheese, salt, and pepper together. Add to beaten eggs and beat until combined.
3. Add noodles to boiling broth, then gradually add egg mixture, stirring constantly. Continue stirring and simmer 5 minutes.
4. Serve topped with parsley.

Roman Egg Soup with Spinach: Follow recipe for

Roman Egg Soup with Noodles; omit noodles. Add ½ **pound chopped cooked fresh spinach** to broth before adding egg mixture.

Italian Chicken Soup Tortellini

8 TO 10
SERVINGS

2 quarts water
1 broiler-fryer chicken
 (about 2½ pounds)
1 onion, sliced
2 teaspoons fresh minced
 parsley or 1 teaspoon dried
 parsley
1½ teaspoons salt
1 teaspoon rosemary or
 chervil
⅛ teaspoon pepper
1 cup sliced celery with
 leaves
1 cup sliced fresh
 mushrooms
½ cup dry white wine
32 tortellini (see recipe)

1. Place water, chicken, onion, parsley, salt, rosemary, and pepper in a large saucepan. Bring to boiling; simmer covered 1 hour, or until chicken is tender.
2. Remove chicken; cool. Discard chicken skin. Remove meat from bones and chop fine. Reserve for tortellini filling.
3. Bring stock to boiling; stir in remaining ingredients. Simmer 15 minutes, or until tortellini are done. (If using frozen tortellini, simmer about 30 minutes.)

Tortellini

ABOUT
128 TORTELLINI

Dough:
2 eggs
2 egg whites
2 tablespoons olive or
 vegetable oil
2 teaspoons salt
3 cups all-purpose flour

Filling:
2½ cups finely chopped
 chicken
¼ cup grated Parmesan
 cheese
2 egg yolks

1. Prepare dough by combining eggs, egg whites, oil, and salt in a bowl. Gradually add flour, mixing well until mixture forms a soft dough. Turn onto a floured surface and knead in remaining flour to form a very stiff dough.
2. Wrap dough in waxed paper; let rest 10 minutes.
3. Combine chicken, cheese, and egg yolks in a bowl. Set aside.
4. Divide dough in quarters. Roll each quarter into a large circle as thin as possible. Cut into about 32 (2-inch) rounds.
5. For each tortellini, place about 1 teaspoon chicken mixture in center of round. Moisten edges with water. Fold in half; seal edges. Shape into rings by stretching the tips of half circle slightly and wrapping the ring around your index finger. Gently press tips together (tortellini may be frozen at this point).
6. Cook as directed in recipe for Chicken Soup Tortellini.

Crispy Breadsticks

32 STICKS

1 cup whole wheat flour
1 package active dry yeast
1 tablespoon sugar
1 teaspoon salt
⅔ cup hot water
2 tablespoons vegetable oil
1 to 1¼ cups all-purpose
 flour

1. Stir together whole wheat flour, yeast, sugar, and salt in a mixing bowl.
2. Blend in water and oil; beat until smooth.
3. Stir in enough flour to form a soft dough.
4. Turn onto a floured surface; continue to work in flour until dough is stiff enough to knead. Knead until smooth and elastic (about 5 minutes), working in as much flour as possible. (The more flour, the crispier the bread sticks.)

(continued)

5. Cover with bowl; let rest about 30 minutes.

6. Divide dough in quarters. Divide each quarter into 8 equal pieces. For ease in shaping, allow dough to rest about 10 minutes. Roll each piece with palms of hands into 10-inch lengths.

7. Place on greased baking sheets about ½ inch apart. If desired, brush with a mixture of 1 egg white and 1 teaspoon water.

8. Bake at 325°F 20 minutes, or until golden brown and crispy.

Italian "Little Hats" in Broth

8 SERVINGS

½ cup (4 ounces) ricotta or cottage cheese
2 tablespoons grated Parmesan cheese
½ cup finely chopped cooked chicken
1 egg, slightly beaten
⅛ teaspoon salt
Few grains nutmeg
Few grains pepper
2 cups sifted all-purpose flour
¼ teaspoon salt
2 eggs
3 tablespoons cold water
2 quarts chicken broth or bouillon

1. Combine cheeses, chicken, 1 egg, ⅛ teaspoon salt, nutmeg, and pepper; set aside.

2. Combine flour and ¼ teaspoon salt in a large bowl. Make a well in the center of the flour. Place 2 eggs, one at a time, in the well, mixing slightly after each one is added. Gradually add the water; mix well to make a stiff dough. Turn dough onto a lightly floured surface and knead until smooth and elastic (5 to 8 minutes).

3. Roll dough out to about 1 inch thick. Cut into 2½-inch circles. Place ½ teaspoon of the chicken-cheese mixture in the center of each round. Dampen the edges with water, fold in half, and press together to seal. Bring the two ends together, dampen, and pinch together.

4. Bring the chicken broth to boiling. Add pasta and cook 20 to 25 minutes, or until pasta is tender. Pour broth and pasta into soup bowls, and serve immediately.

Italian White Bean Soup

8 TO 10 SERVINGS

2 cups (about ½ pound) dried navy beans, soaked overnight
2 quarts water
2 cups chopped potato (about 1 large)
1 can (16 ounces) tomatoes (undrained)
¼ cup chopped onion
2 teaspoons salt
1 clove garlic, crushed
1 teaspoon crushed basil
1 cup (about 2 ounces) broken vermicelli or shell macaroni

1. Combine in a large saucepan beans, water, potato, tomatoes, onions, salt, garlic, and basil. Bring to boiling; simmer 1 hour, or until beans are tender.

2. Stir in vermicelli; cook 20 minutes.

Egg and Lemon Soup

Greek Egg-Lemon Soup

4 TO 6
SERVINGS

6 cups rich veal or chicken broth (page 62) or 6 bouillon cubes in 6 cups water
⅓ cup uncooked rice
3 eggs
¼ cup lemon juice

1. Bring broth to boiling in a large saucepan. Add rice; cover and simmer until rice is tender, about 20 minutes.
2. Beat eggs until frothy in a bowl; add lemon juice. Beat in 2 cups of broth very slowly; stir the mixture into the remaining soup.
3. Heat to serving temperature, being very careful not to let it boil (boiling will curdle the egg).

Suggested accompaniment: Pita (page 34).

Greek Egg and Lemon Soup with Sour-Dough Noodles

ABOUT
2½ CUPS

1½ quarts chicken broth
1 cup trahana (see Note)
Salt and pepper to taste
2 eggs, separated
Juice of 2 lemons

1. Bring broth to boiling; boil 6 minutes. Add trahana, salt, and pepper. Simmer covered 10 minutes.
2. In a small bowl, using a wire whisk, beat egg whites until frothy. In another bowl, beat egg yolks. Combine. Slowly beat in lemon juice, then 1 cup hot broth. Add to soup. Serve immediately.

Note: There are three varieties of trahana dough — sour, sweet, sweet-sour. It may be made at home (see recipe for Sweet-Sour Trahana page 34) or purchased at a Greek grocery store.

Pita

EIGHT
8-INCH LOAVES

7½ to 8 cups all-purpose
    flour
2 packages active dry yeast
2 tablespoons sugar
2 teaspoons salt
2½ cups hot water
    (120°–130°F)
¼ cup olive or vegetable oil
1 cup cornmeal

1. Combine 2 cups flour, yeast, sugar, and salt in a large mixing bowl.
2. Stir in water and oil; beat until smooth.
3. Stir in enough remaining flour to make a soft dough.
4. Turn out onto a floured surface; continue to work in flour until dough is stiff enough to knead. Knead until smooth and elastic (about 5 minutes).
5. Place in an oiled bowl; turn to oil top of dough. Cover; let rise in a warm place until double in bulk (about 45 minutes).
6. Punch dough down and divide into 8 equal parts. Roll each into a ball. Let dough rest 5 minutes. Roll 4 of the balls into 8-inch rounds, ⅛ inch thick. Sprinkle 2 greased baking sheets with cornmeal. Place rounds on baking sheets. Cover; let rise 30 minutes. (See Note.)
7. Bake at 450°F 8 to 10 minutes, or until puffed and brown. Prepare the 4 remaining loaves in the same manner.

Note: Be careful when handling the dough not to crease or pinch it, or the pockets won't form.

Sweet-Sour Trahana

2 eggs, slightly beaten
½ cup plain yogurt
½ cup milk
1 teaspoon salt
1½ cups all-purpose flour
Semolina (about 1½ cups)

1. Blend eggs, yogurt, milk, and salt. Add flour and semolina, a little at a time, to form a stiff dough.
2. Knead for about 5 minutes (dough will be very sticky). Divide into small portions. Roll with hands into balls. Place on a clean cloth.
3. Flatten each piece as thin as possible. Let dry undisturbed on trivets at least 12 hours.
4. Cut into small pieces. Turn pieces over and continue drying for another 12 hours or more.
5. When completely dry, mash into crumbs with rolling pin. Spread on a baking sheet.
6. Bake at 200°F for 2 hours.

Note: The weather affects the drying of the trahana. When it is humid, allow more time for drying. Homemade trahana is far superior to the commercially made product. Store in an airtight jar indefinitely.

Sweet Trahana: Follow recipe for Sweet-Sour Trahana; omit yogurt and increase milk to 1 cup.

Sour Trahana: Follow recipe for Sweet-Sour Trahana; omit milk and increase yogurt to 1 cup.

French Onion Soup

6 SERVINGS

5 medium onions, sliced
(4 cups)
3 tablespoons butter or
margarine
1½ quarts beef broth
½ teaspoon salt
⅛ teaspoon pepper
Cheese Croutons (see recipe
below)

1. Sauté onions in melted butter in a large saucepan. Cook slowly, stirring until golden (about 10 minutes).
2. Blend in beef broth, salt, and pepper. Bring to boiling, cover, and simmer 15 minutes.
3. Pour soup into warm soup bowls or crocks. Float a cheese crouton in each bowl of soup.

Cheese Croutons

6 slices French bread,
toasted
2 tablespoons butter or
margarine
¼ cup (1 ounce) grated
Gruyère or Swiss cheese

1. Spread one side of each bread slice with butter. If necessary, cut bread to fit size of bowl. Sprinkle cheese over buttered toast.
2. Place under broiler until cheese melts.

Onion Soup Les Halles

ABOUT
1 QUART

2 tablespoons butter
2 large onions, coarsely
chopped
1 clove garlic, finely chopped
½ teaspoon salt
⅛ teaspoon black pepper
⅛ teaspoon thyme
1 large sprig parsley,
snipped
2 teaspoons tarragon vinegar
1 can (10½ ounces) con-
densed beef consommé
1⅓ cups water
1 can (12 ounces) cocktail
vegetable juice

1. Heat butter in a saucepan; add onions and garlic and cook about 5 minutes.
2. Stir in salt, pepper, thyme, parsley, vinegar, consommé, water, and vegetable juice. Simmer about 10 minutes.
3. Serve piping hot, floating a **buttered toast round,** topped with **shredded Parmesan cheese,** in each bowl of soup.

French Cottage Sprout Soup

ABOUT
2½ QUARTS

2 packages (10 ounces each)
frozen Brussels sprouts
½ cup butter or margarine
¼ cup flour
1 teaspoon salt
½ teaspoon pepper
4 cups chicken broth
(dissolve 4 chicken bouillon
cubes in 4 cups boiling
water)
½ pound fresh mushrooms
2 cups light cream

1. Cook Brussels sprouts according to package directions, using ½ teaspoon salt to 1 cup water; drain, if necessary.
2. Meanwhile, heat butter in a large heavy saucepan. Blend in a mixture of the flour, salt, and pepper; cook until bubbly. Gradually add the broth, stirring to blend. Bring to boiling; stir and boil 1 minute. Remove from heat.
3. Finely chop mushrooms in an electric blender. Mix mushrooms into hot sauce; cover and simmer 20 minutes.
4. In the blender, purée one half of the sprouts with 1 cup cream. Pour into cooked mushroom sauce. Repeat with remaining Brussels sprouts and cream.
5. Heat the soup, stirring occasionally, until of serving temperature. Garnish with **parsley.**

French Cauliflower Soup

6 SERVINGS

1 head cauliflower, cut in
flowerets
5 cups chicken stock or 5
chicken bouillon cubes in 5
cups water
½ cup uncooked rice
¼ cup finely chopped celery
1 cup milk or half-and-half
¼ cup flour
Salt and pepper
Sliced green onion, snipped
watercress, or snipped
parsley

1. Put cauliflowerets, stock, rice, and celery into a large saucepan. Bring to boiling; simmer until cauliflower is crisp-tender and rice is cooked (about 10 minutes).
2. Gradually add milk to flour, blending until smooth; stir into soup. Bring to boiling, stirring constantly until thickened. Season to taste.
3. Sprinkle each serving with green onion, watercress, or parsley.

Creamed French Cauliflower Soup: Follow recipe for French Cauliflower Soup; strain soup after Step 1. Purée vegetables and rice in an electric blender. Return vegetables and stock to saucepot. Continue with Step 2. Stir in ¼ **cup white wine** and either ½ **teaspoon basil** or ¼ **teaspoon dill weed.** Garnish as suggested.

Pea Soup A la Française

6 SERVINGS

1 small head lettuce, shredded (about 5 cups)
2 cups shelled fresh green
peas, or one 10-ounce
package frozen green peas
1 cup water
½ cup chopped leek (white
and green)
2 tablespoons butter
2 teaspoons chervil
1 teaspoon sugar
1 teaspoon salt
¼ teaspoon black pepper
1 can (10½ ounces) condensed beef broth
¾ cup water
2 cups light cream

1. Put the lettuce, peas, 1 cup water, leek, butter, chervil, sugar, salt, and pepper into a large saucepan; stir and bring to boiling. Cover and cook until peas are tender.
2. Press mixture through a coarse sieve or food mill and return to saucepan. Stir in beef broth and ¾ cup water.
3. Just before serving, stir cream into mixture and heat thoroughly.

Soup Mexicana

6 TO 8
SERVINGS

1 chicken breast
6 cups chicken broth
2 onions, chopped
1 teaspoon monosodium
glutamate
1 tablespoon butter or
margarine
1½ teaspoons grated onion
2 cups chopped zucchini
1 cup drained canned whole
kernel corn
⅓ cup tomato purée
2 ounces cream cheese, cut
in small cubes
2 avocados, sliced

1. Cook chicken breast 30 minutes, or until tender, in the broth with the chopped onion and monosodium glutamate. Remove chicken; dice and set aside. Reserve broth.
2. Heat butter and grated onion in a large saucepan; blend in zucchini and corn. Cook about 5 minutes, stirring occasionally. Mix in the broth and tomato purée. Cover and simmer about 20 minutes.
3. Just before serving, mix in diced chicken, cream cheese, and avocados.

Note: Any remaining soup may be stored, covered, in the refrigerator.

Volhynian Beef Soup from Poland

ABOUT
2½ QUARTS

¼ cup dried navy or pea
  beans
2 cups water
2 cups Bread Kvas (below)
2 cups meat broth, bouillon,
  or meat stock
6 medium beets, cooked and
  peeled
1 can (16 ounces) tomatoes
  (undrained)
1 small head cabbage (about
  1½ pounds)
1 small sour apple
Salt and pepper
1 tablespoon butter
  (optional)
Sour cream

1. Bring beans and water just to boiling in a large kettle. Remove from heat. Let stand 1 hour. Then boil for 20 minutes, or until beans are tender. Add kvas and meat broth.
2. Slice beets. Mash tomatoes or make a purée by pressing through a sieve or using an electric blender. Add beets and tomatoes to beans.
3. Cut cabbage into sixths; remove core. Pare apple, if desired; core and dice. Add cabbage and apple to beans.
4. Season to taste with salt and pepper. Stir in butter, if desired. Cook soup over medium heat 30 minutes.
5. To serve, spoon a small amount of sour cream into each bowl. Ladle in hot soup and stir.

Bread Kvas

ABOUT
3 CUPS

1 quart hot water
1 pound beets, pared and sliced
1 rye bread crust

1. Pour hot water over beets in a casserole. Add bread. Cover with a cloth. Let stand 3 to 4 days.
2. Drain off clear juice and use as a base for soup.

Crème Senegalese

ABOUT
2 QUARTS

2 tablespoons butter or
  margarine
2 stalks celery, finely
  chopped
2 tablespoons grated onion
1 to 2 tablespoons curry
  powder
2 tablespoons flour
2 quarts chicken broth,
  cooled
½ cup finely cut fresh
  pineapple
1 canned pineapple slice,
  finely cut
1½ cups finely diced cooked
  chicken
2 cups cream

1. Heat butter in a large saucepan. Add celery and onion; cover and cook until celery is tender, stirring occasionally; remove from heat.
2. Blend curry powder and flour in a bowl; slowly add 1 cup of the chicken broth, stirring until smooth after each addition.
3. Adding gradually and stirring constantly, pour into mixture in saucepan. Bring to boiling; continue cooking 5 minutes, stirring constantly.
4. Continue stirring and gradually add remaining broth; simmer, uncovered, 30 minutes, stirring occasionally.
5. Remove from heat; sieve mixture. Stir in the fresh and canned pineapple and the diced chicken. Cool soup.
6. Blend cream into cooled soup; chill thoroughly.
7. Top each serving of chilled soup with **whipped cream.**

Lebanon Lentil Soup

8 SERVINGS

2 quarts beef broth
1 ham bone
1¼ cups (about ½ pound)
  lentils
2 stalks celery, sliced
2 carrots, sliced
1 onion, sliced
1 teaspoon salt
¼ teaspoon pepper
½ teaspoon crushed thyme
  or ¼ teaspoon dill
  weed

1. Combine all ingredients in a large saucepan. Bring to boiling. Cover; simmer 1 to 2 hours, or until lentils are tender.
2. Remove ham bone. Force soup mixture through a coarse sieve or food mill, or purée in an electric blender.
3. Heat, if necessary.

Cream of Lentil Soup: Follow recipe for Lebanon Lentil Soup. After puréeing, stir in 1 cup half-and-half or whipping cream.

Cuban Black Bean Soup

ABOUT
2 QUARTS

1 pound black beans, washed
2 quarts boiling water
2 tablespoons salt
5 cloves garlic
1½ teaspoons cumin
1½ teaspoons white vinegar
10 tablespoons olive oil
½ pound onions, peeled,
  trimmed, and chopped
½ pound green peppers,
  peeled, trimmed, and
  chopped

1. Put beans into a large heavy saucepot or Dutch oven and add boiling water; boil rapidly 2 minutes. Cover tightly, remove from heat, and set aside 1 hour. Add salt to beans and liquid; bring to boiling and simmer, covered, until beans are soft.
2. Put the garlic, cumin, oregano, and vinegar into a mortar and crush to a paste.
3. Heat olive oil in a large skillet. Mix in onion and green pepper and fry until onion is browned, stirring occasionally. Thoroughly blend in the paste, then stir the skillet mixture into the beans. cook over low heat until ready to serve.
4. Meanwhile, mix a small portion of **cooked rice, minced onion, olive oil,** and **vinegar** in a bowl, set aside to marinate. Add a soup spoon of rice mixture to each serving of soup.

Note: For a combination soup and salad course served before the entrée, set out chilled ripe **avocado halves** and spoon the piping hot bean soup into the cavities. (The blend of flavors is subtle, elegant, and distinctive.)

Hungarian Goulash Soup

4 TO 6
SERVINGS

1½ pounds beef for stew, cut
  into ½-inch cubes
1 tablespoon shortening or
  vegetable oil
1 large onion, chopped
1 quart water
¾ cup grated potato (about
  1 large)
1 tablespoon paprika
1 tablespoon tomato sauce
  or ketchup
1 teaspoon salt
½ teaspoon caraway seed
  (optional)
¼ teaspoon crushed thyme
Pinch red pepper
1 cup chopped pared raw
  potato (about 1 large)
1 cup uncooked egg noodles

1. Brown meat in shortening in a large saucepan. Add onion; cook until tender.
2. Add water, grated potato, and seasonings. Bring to boiling; cover. Simmer 1½ hours, or until beef is tender.
3. Stir in potatoes and noodles. Cook until tender, 10 to 20 minutes.

Hungarian Goulash Soup with Spaetzle: Follow recipe for Hungarian Goulash Soup, omitting chopped potato and noodles. Serve with **hot buttered spaetzle** (below).

Suggested accompaniment: Peasant Black Bread (page 39).

Spaetzle

2 cups all-purpose flour
1 teaspoon salt
1 egg
¼ to ½ cup water

1. Combine flour and salt; stir in egg. Gradually add water until batter is stiff, but smooth. Place on wet cutting board; flatten.
2. With a wet knife, scrape small pieces of dough off and drop into boiling salted water. Cook only one layer of spaetzle at a time, boiling gently 5 to 8 minutes, or until done. Remove with perforated spoon.

Note: Spaetzle may be served in pea, lentil, or tomato soup or as a side dish, either tossed with hot melted butter or sautéed in butter. For variety, sprinkle with toasted bread crumbs or grated Parmesan cheese.

Peasant Black Bread

Peasant Black Bread

2 LOAVES

3½ cups rye flour
½ cup unsweetened cocoa
¼ cup sugar
3 tablespoons caraway seed
2 packages active dry yeast
1 tablespoon instant coffee
(powder or crystals)
2 teaspoons salt
2½ cups hot water (120°-
130°F)
¼ cup vinegar
¼ cup dark molasses
¼ cup vegetable oil or
melted butter
3½ to 4½ cups unbleached
or all-purpose flour

1. Thoroughly mix rye flour, cocoa, sugar, caraway, yeast, coffee, and salt in a large mixing bowl.
2. Stir in water, vinegar, molasses, and oil; beat until smooth.
3. Stir in enough unbleached flour to make a soft dough.
4. Turn onto a floured surface. Knead until smooth and elastic (about 5 minutes).
5. Place in an oiled bowl; turn to oil top of dough. Cover; let rise in warm place until doubled (about 1 hour).
6. Punch dough down. Divide in half; shape each half into a ball and place in center of 2 greased 8-inch round cake pans. Cover; let rise until double in bulk (about 1 hour).
7. Bake at 350°F 40 to 45 minutes, or until done.

Dutch-Style Chowder

4 slices bacon, diced
⅓ cup chopped onion
1 can (10½ ounces)
condensed cream of
chicken soup
1 can (10½ ounces) con-
densed chicken-vegetable
soup
1 soup can milk
1 soup can water
1 cup drained canned whole
kernel corn
2 tablespoons snipped
parsley

1. Cook bacon in a saucepan until crisp. Remove from pan to absorbent paper.
2. Pour off all except 1 tablespoon fat from pan. Add onion and cook until tender and lightly browned, stirring occasionally.
3. Stir in the soups, milk, water, and corn. Heat thoroughly, stirring frequently.

Chinese Chicken-Mushroom Soup

5 SERVINGS

1 pound chicken breasts
½ teaspoon salt
1 tablespoon cooking oil
10 medium-size mushrooms, sliced
4 chicken bouillon cubes
4 cups hot water
1 tablespoon cornstarch
3 tablespoons cold water
1 tablespoon soy sauce
2 tablespoons lemon juice

1. Bone chicken breasts, remove skin, and cut into ¼-inch-wide strips, 1½ to 2 inches long. Sprinkle with salt and let stand 30 minutes.
2. Heat oil in a wok and sauté mushrooms a few minutes until golden. Remove from wok. Dissolve bouillon cubes in hot water and set aside.
3. Mix cornstarch with cold water. Stir in soy sauce. Combine with chicken bouillon in the wok. Bring to boiling, add chicken pieces, and simmer, covered, 5 minutes.
4. Add mushrooms and lemon juice to soup, adding more salt, if necessary. Heat gently without boiling.
5. Serve with a thin **lemon slice** in each bowl.

Chinese Beef Sub Gum Soup

ABOUT
6 SERVINGS

½ pound beef round, cut into small cubes
1 tablespoon cooking oil
1 can (20 ounces) Chinese vegetables, drained
2 cans (10½ ounces each) condensed beef broth or bouillon
2 cups water
¼ cup uncooked rice
2 tablespoons soy sauce
⅛ teaspoon pepper
1 egg, beaten

1. In a large wok, brown beef in hot oil. Chop vegetables and add to the browned meat with remaining ingredients, except egg.
2. Bring soup to boiling, stirring to blend. Cover and simmer 40 minutes.
3. Remove soup from heat and slowly stir in the egg. Let stand until egg is set.

New Orleans Gumbo

8 SERVINGS

2 onions, chopped
½ cup butter or margarine
¼ cup flour
2 quarts chicken stock
1 can (28 ounces) tomatoes
½ pound okra, sliced
1 stalk celery, sliced
½ teaspoon thyme
1 bay leaf
½ teaspoon salt
Pinch pepper
Pinch cayenne pepper
6 hard-shell crabs
24 large peeled and deveined shrimp
24 oysters
2 cups cooked rice

1. Sauté onion in butter in a large saucepan. Mix in flour; cook until bubbly.
2. Gradually add chicken stock, tomatoes, okra, celery, and seasonings; add crabs. Simmer 1 hour.
3. Add shrimp and oysters; simmer 5 minutes.
4. Put ¼ cup rice into each soup bowl; ladle in hot gumbo.

Chinese Chicken-Mushroom Soup

Mulligatawny Soup from India

ABOUT
8 SERVINGS

1 broiler-fryer chicken (2½
   to 3 pounds), cut in pieces
1 package soup greens (or
   see Note)
1 onion, peeled and
   quartered
1 teaspoon salt
1 bay leaf
1 cup water
5 thick slices lean bacon,
   diced
4 tomatoes, peeled and
   chopped
⅓ cup flour
2 teaspoons curry powder
Cayenne pepper
½ cup half-and-half

1. Put chicken, soup greens, onion, salt, bay leaf, and water
into an electric cooker.
2. Cover and cook on Low 4 hours.
3. Remove chicken from cooker and set aside. Strain broth
and reserve 1 cup. Pour remaining broth into cooker.
4. Fry bacon in a skillet until lightly browned. Add chopped
tomato and cook 2 minutes. Stir in flour and curry powder.
Add reserved chicken broth gradually, stirring constantly until mixture comes to boiling. Add to broth in cooker.
5. Remove chicken meat from skin and bones and cut in
strips. Add to cooker; stir.
6. Cover and cook on High 2 hours.
7. Add cayenne and half-and-half to cooker; mix well.
8. Serve soup with **toasted bread cubes.**

Note: For soup greens, use all or a choice of the following
vegetables: carrot, celery, leek, onion, parsnip, turnip; and
herbs: parsley, tarragon, thyme.

Suggested accompaniment: Indian Flat Bread.

Mulligatawny Soup

Indian Flat Bread

16 ROUND
LOAVES

1 cup all-purpose flour
1 package active dry yeast
2 teaspoons salt
1 cup hot water (120°-
   130°F)
¼ cup buttermilk or yogurt
1 egg (at room temperature)
2 tablespoons vegetable oil
1 tablespoon honey or sugar
2 to 3 cups all-purpose flour
Melted butter (optional)
Cornmeal or sesame or poppy seeds (optional)

1. Combine 1 cup flour, yeast, and salt in a mixing bowl.
2. Stir in water, buttermilk, egg, oil, and honey; beat until
smooth.
3. Stir in enough remaining flour to form a soft, sticky
dough.
4. Turn onto a floured surface; continue to work in flour
until dough is stiff enough to knead. Knead until smooth
and elastic, but still soft (3 to 5 minutes).
5. Place in an oiled bowl, turning once to oil top of dough.
Cover; let rise until double in bulk (about 45 minutes).
6. Punch dough down. Shape into 16 equal balls. Let rest
5 minutes. Roll out each ball to a ¼-inch-thick round. If
desired, brush with melted butter and sprinkle with cornmeal, sesame, or poppy seeds. Set on baking sheets.
7. Bake at 450°F 5 to 8 minutes.

SOUPS FOR SPECIAL OCCASIONS

Harvest Soup

ABOUT
20 SERVINGS

8 slices bacon, cut in 1- to
2-inches pieces
2 cloves garlic, minced
5 cups chicken broth
(dissolve 7 chicken bouillon
cubes in 5 cups boiling
water)
6 cups milk
¾ cup uncooked rice
1 teaspoon oregano, crushed
2 teaspoons salt
½ teaspoon black pepper
1 package (10 ounces) frozen
peas and carrots
2 cups water
4 packages (10 ounces each)
frozen Brussels sprouts,
partially thawed and
quartered
¾ cup shredded Parmesan
cheese

1. Fry bacon with garlic in a large saucepot or Dutch oven until bacon is partially cooked.
2. And 3 cups of the broth, the milk, rice, and a mixture of the oregano, 1 teaspoon salt, and pepper. Bring to boiling, reduce heat and simmer, covered, 15 minutes.
3. Add peas and carrots; bring to boiling, reduce heat and simmer about 10 minutes, or until tender.
4. Meanwhile, combine remaining broth, salt, and water in a saucepan. Bring to boiling and add Brussels sprouts. Return to boiling and simmer, uncovered, 10 minutes, or until tender.
5. Add Brussels sprouts with their cooking liquid to rice mixture. Stir in cheese.

Zuppa di Pesce: Royal Danieli

ABOUT
2½ QUARTS
SOUP

3 pounds skinned and boned
fish (haddock, trout, cod,
salmon, and red snapper)
1 lobster (about 1 pound)
1 pound shrimp with shells
1 quart water
½ cup coarsely cut onion
1 stalk celery with leaves,
coarsely cut
2 tablespoons cider vinegar
2 teaspoons salt
¼ cup olive oil
2 cloves garlic, minced
1 bay leaf, crumbled
1 teaspoon basil
½ teaspoon thyme
2 tablespoons minced parsley
½ to 1 cup dry white wine
½ cup chopped peeled
tomatoes
8 shreds saffron
1 teaspoon salt
½ teaspoon freshly ground
black pepper
6 slices French bread
¼ cup olive oil

1. Reserve heads and tails of fish. Cut fish into bite-size pieces.
2. In a saucepot or kettle, boil lobster and shrimp 5 minutes in water with onion, celery, vinegar, and 2 teaspoons salt.
3. Remove and shell lobster and shrimp; devein shrimp. Cut lobster into bite-size pieces. Set lobster and shrimp aside.
4. Return shells to the broth and add heads and tails of fish. Simmer 20 minutes.
5. Strain broth, pour into saucepot, and set aside.
6. Sauté all of the fish in ¼ cup oil with garlic, bay leaf, basil, thyme, and parsley 5 minutes, stirring constantly.
7. Add to reserved broth along with wine, tomatoes, saffron, 1 teaspoon salt, and the pepper. Bring to boiling; cover and simmer 10 minutes, stirring occasionally.
8. Serve with slices of bread sautéed in the remaining ¼ cup olive oil.

Rock Lobster Bouillabaisse

6 SERVINGS

¼ cup olive oil
1 cup chopped celery
1 onion, chopped
1 clove garlic, chopped
½ teaspoon thyme
1 bay leaf
1 can (28 ounces) tomatoes (undrained)
1 bottle (8 ounces) clam juice
1 cup dry white wine
¼ cup chopped parsley
1½ pounds fish fillets (turbot, flounder, cod, or halibut), cut in 2-inch pieces
1 pound frozen South African rock lobster tails
Salt and pepper

1. Heat olive oil in a saucepot and sauté celery, onion, and garlic until tender but not brown. Add thyme, bay leaf, tomatoes, clam juice, wine, and parsley. Cover and simmer 15 minutes.
2. Add fish to saucepot. Cut each frozen rock lobster tail into 3 pieces, crosswise through hard shell, and add to stew. Simmer 10 minutes.
3. Season to taste with salt and pepper. Remove bay leaf.
4. Ladle into large bowls and serve with slices of **French bread.**

Crab Meat Bisque

8 SERVINGS

½ cup chopped onion
⅓ cup chopped carrot
1 leek (white part only), minced
3 tablespoons butter or margarine
1 quart White Stock (see page 68)
1 teaspoon salt
⅛ teaspoon pepper
1 bay leaf
3 egg yolks, beaten
1 cup whipping cream
½ cup dry white wine
2 cups (8 ounces) flaked fresh crab meat
Minced parsley

1. Sauté onion, carrot, and leek in melted butter in a large saucepan. Stir in white stock, salt, pepper, and bay leaf. Cover; simmer 10 minutes.
2. Push mixture through sieve or food mill or purée in an electric blender. Return to saucepan.
3. Stir about 3 tablespoons hot soup into egg yolks. Return mixture to soup, stirring constantly.
4. Stir in whipping cream, wine, and crab meat. Heat; do not boil.
5. Sprinkle parsley over each serving.

Lobster Bisque: Follow recipe for Crab Meat Bisque, substituting **2 cans (about 6 ounces each) lobster meat,** drained, for the crab meat.

Shrimp Bisque: Follow recipe for Crab Meat Bisque, substituting **2½ cups chopped cooked shrimp** for crab meat.

Oyster Bisque Antoine

ABOUT 1½ QUARTS SOUP

2 tablespoons minced celery
2 tablespoons butter
3 tablespoons flour
¾ teaspoon salt
⅛ teaspoon white pepper
1 quart milk, scalded
2 cups oysters
¾ cup heavy cream, scalded
2 tablespoons sherry

1. In a heavy saucepan, cook the celery in butter until yellow in color. Stir in the flour, salt, and pepper; cook until bubbly. Blend in the scalded milk, cooking and stirring until thickened and smooth.
2. Heat the oysters in their liquor until the edges curl. Drain and reserve the liquor. Finely chop the oysters and rub them through a fine sieve or purée oysters in a blender.
3. Add the oysters to the white sauce alternately with the cream. Add sherry. (If bisque seems too thick, thin it with some of the oyster liquor.)

Rock Lobster Bouillabaise

Creamy Shrimp and Avocado Bisque

10 SERVINGS

2 cans (about 10 ounces each) condensed cream of asparagus soup
2 cans (about 10 ounces each) condensed cream of potato soup
1 teaspoon curry powder
2 soup cans milk
2 soup cans half-and-half
2 cups cooked shrimp, cut in pieces (see Note)
1 avocado, peeled and chopped
2 tablespoons minced chives

1. Combine soups and curry in a large, heavy saucepan. Stir in milk and half-and-half. Set over low heat until thoroughly heated, stirring occasionally.
2. Mix in shrimp; heat thoroughly; do not boil.
3. Pour into soup tureen; gently stir in avocado. Sprinkle with chives. Serve at once.

Note: When using fresh or fresh-frozen shrimp, shell and devein. To remove the vein, make a shallow cut lengthwise down the back of each shrimp. Remove vein with point of knife.

Cool and Creamy Shrimp and Avocado Bisque: Follow recipe for Creamy Shrimp and Avocado Bisque; chill before serving.

Toasted Almond Soup

5 OR 6 SERVINGS

1 cup water
1 cup salted roasted almonds
4 egg yolks
3 chicken bouillon cubes
1 small slice onion
½ teaspoon sugar
2 cups water
1 cup half-and-half

1. Put 1 cup water, almonds, egg yolks, bouillon cubes, onion, and sugar in an electric blender container. Blend until almonds are finely ground.
2. Pour into a saucepan; stir in 2 cups water. Cook over low heat about 5 minutes, or until mixture coats a spoon, stirring constantly (do not boil).
3. Stir in half-and-half and heat thoroughly without boiling. Garnish with **finely shredded orange peel.**

Pacific Seafood Chowder

ABOUT 8 SERVINGS

1½ pounds North Pacific halibut, fresh or frozen
1 can (7½ ounces) Alaska King crab or 1 package (6 ounces) frozen Alaska King crab
3 medium potatoes
1 large sweet Spanish onion
¾ cup chopped celery
¼ cup chopped green pepper
2 cloves garlic, minced
¼ cup butter or margarine
2 cans (16 ounces each) tomatoes
2 cups clam-tomato juice
1½ teaspoons salt
¼ teaspoon pepper
¼ teaspoon thyme
¼ teaspoon marjoram
1 dozen small hard-shell clams
Snipped parsley

1. Defrost halibut, if frozen. Cut into 1-inch chunks. Drain canned crab and slice. Or defrost, drain, and slice frozen crab. Pare potatoes and cut into ½-inch pieces. Peel and thinly slice onion.
2. Sauté onion, celery, green pepper, and garlic in butter in a saucepot. Add tomatoes with liquid, clam-tomato juice, and seasonings. Cover and simmer 30 minutes. Add halibut, potatoes, and clams. Cover and simmer about 10 minutes, or until halibut and potatoes are done and clam shells open. Add crab and heat through.
3. Sprinkle with parsley. Serve with buttered crusty bread.

**Pacific
Seafood
Chowder**

Salmon Chowder

8 TO 10
SERVINGS

3 tablespoons butter
½ cup chopped onion
2 tablespoons chopped green
  pepper
1 can (10½ ounces) conensed
  cream of celery soup
3 cups milk
1 can (16 ounces) pink
  salmon, drained, skin and
  bones discarded, and meat
  separated in chunks
1½ cups diced pared
  potatoes, cooked
1 cup diced pared carrots,
  cooked
1 can (16 ounces) tomatoes,
  drained
1 teaspoon salt
½ teaspoon monosodium
  glutamate
¼ teaspoon pepper

1. Heat butter in a large saucepan. Add onion and green pepper; cook until tender.
2. Stir in soup and milk. Mix in salmon and remaining ingredients. Heat thoroughly, stirring occasionally (do not boil).
3. Ladle chowder into heated soup bowls and serve immediately.

Sherried Chicken Chowder

8 SERVINGS

10 cups water
1 broiler-fryer chicken
  (about 2½ pounds)
1 carrot, coarsely chopped
1 stalk celery, coarsely
  chopped
1 onion, halved
4 whole cloves
2 teaspoons salt
1 teaspoon crushed tarragon
1 bay leaf
½ cup uncooked barley or
  rice
½ teaspoon curry powder
¼ cup dry sherry
1 cup half-and-half

1. Place water, chicken, carrot, celery, onion halves studded with cloves, salt, and tarragon in Dutch oven or saucepot. Bring to boiling; simmer 1 hour, or until chicken is tender.
2. Remove chicken; cool. Discard skin; remove meat from bones; chop.
3. Strain stock. Discard cloves and bay leaf. Reserve stock and vegetables. Skim fat from stock.
4. Purée vegetables and 1 cup stock in an electric blender.
5. Return stock to Dutch oven; bring to boiling. Stir in barley and puréed vegetables. Simmer 1 hour, or until barley is tender. Stir in chicken, curry, sherry, and half-and-half.

Oyster Stew

4 SERVINGS

¼ cup butter or margarine
1 pint fresh oysters,
  drained; reserve liquor
1½ cups milk
1 cup half-and-half
1 teaspoon salt
Pinch black pepper or
  cayenne pepper
Minced parsley

1. Melt butter in a saucepan. Add milk, half-and-half, and oyster liquor. Scald; do not boil
2. Add oysters and seasonings. Heat; do not boil.
3. Garnish with parsley.

COLD SOUPS

Jellied Consommé Madrilène

4 TO 6 SERVINGS

3 cups tomato juice
1 cup strong chicken broth (dissolve 2 chicken bouillon cubes in 1 cup boiling water)
½ cup chopped green pepper
1 teaspoon sugar
2 envelopes unflavored gelatin
¾ cup cold water
2 teaspoons lemon juice
2 teaspoons Angostura bitters

1. Blend in a saucepan the tomato juice, chicken broth, green pepper, and sugar. Cover and simmer 6 to 8 minutes, or until green pepper is tender.
2. Soften gelatin in the cold water in a bowl.
3. Strain tomato juice mixture into bowl with gelatin and stir until dissolved. Blend in the lemon juice and bitters. Cool. Chill until firm.
4. Just before serving, stir mixture lightly with a fork. Spoon into chilled bowls. Garnish servings with notched slices of **lemon,** if desired.

Chilled Dilled Chicken Soup

ABOUT 6 SERVINGS

2 cans (about 10 ounces each) condensed cream of chicken soup
2 soup cans milk
2 teaspoons chopped green onion with tops
½ cup chopped cucumber
2 teaspoons chopped fresh dill or ½ teaspoon dill weed

1. Mix soup and milk in a bowl; blend in the remaining ingredients.
2. Cover and refrigerate 3 to 4 hours to allow flavors to blend.
3. Serve soup thoroughly chilled, or heat and serve.

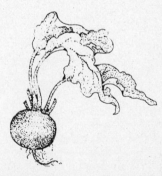

Jellied Borsch

ABOUT 1½ QUARTS

1 can (10½ ounces) condensed consommé
1 cup can water
½ clove garlic
2 stalks celery, cut in pieces
1 tablespoon brown sugar
¼ teaspoon ground ginger
⅛ teaspoon cayenne pepper
1 jar (16 ounces) pickled sliced beets, drained (reserve liquid)
1½ envelopes unflavored gelatin
¼ cup lemon juice
1 cup dairy sour cream

1. Heat consommé and water to boiling in a saucepan. Stir in garlic, celery, brown sugar, ginger, and cayenne pepper. Remove from heat, cover, and let stand 30 minutes.
2. Meanwhile, soften gelatin in resered beet liquid in a saucepan. Stir over low heat until gelatin is completely dissolved.
3. Strain the consommé; stir in dissolved gelatin. Chill until the consistency of unbeaten egg white, stirring occasionally.
4. Put beets and lemon juice into an electric blender container. Cover and blend thoroughly. Add to gelatin mixture along with the sour cream; blend thorouhly.
5. Pour into a shallow 3-quart dish; depth of mixture will be about ¾ inch. Chill until firm.
6. To serve, cut into cubes. Spoon into bouillon cups and garnish each with **dairy sour cream.**

Vichyssoise

8 SERVINGS

4 to 6 leeks
2 tablespoons butter or margarine
4 potatoes, pared and sliced
1 quart chicken broth or 6 chicken bouillon cubes dissolved in 1 quart boiling water
1 cup half-and-half
1 cup chilled whipping cream
Snipped chives

1. Finely slice the white part and about an inch of the green part of each leek to measure about 1 cup.
2. Sauté leeks in butter in a heavy saucepan. Stir in potatoes and broth; bring to boiling. Simmer 40 minutes, or until potatoes are tender.
3. Sieve the cooked vegetables or blend until smooth in an electric blender. Mix in half-and-half; chill thoroughly.
4. Just before serving, stir in whipping cream. Garnish with chives.

Frosty Cucumber Soup

4 SERVINGS

1 large cucumber, scored with a fork
¼ teaspoon salt
Pinch white pepper
1½ cups yogurt
1¼ cups water
½ cup walnuts, ground in an electric blender
2 cloves garlic, minced
Green food coloring (optional)

1. Halve cucumber lengthwise and cut crosswise into very thin slices. Rub inside of a large bowl with cut surface of ½ clove garlic. Combine cucumber, salt, and pepper in bowl. Cover; chill.
2. Pour combined yogurt and water over chilled cucumber; mix well. If desired, tint with 1 or 2 drops of food coloring. Chill.
3. Combine walnuts and garlic; set aside for topping.
4. Ladle soup into bowls. Place soup bowls over larger bowls of crushed ice. Serve with walnut topping.

Cold Cucumber-Beet Soup

ABOUT
2 QUARTS

1 small bunch beets with beet greens (about 1 pound)
1½ quarts water or chicken broth
1 teaspoon salt
2 medium cucumbers, pared and diced
6 radishes, sliced
6 green onions with tops, sliced
2 tablespoons fresh lemon juice
2 cups sour cream or buttermilk
1 dill pickle, minced (optional)
3 tablespoons chopped fresh dill or 4 teaspoons dill weed
Salt and pepper
1 lemon, sliced
2 hard-cooked eggs, chopped or sliced
12 large shrimp, cooked, peeled, and deveined (optional)

1. Scrub beets and carefully wash greens. Leave beets whole; do not peel. Put beets and greens into a kettle with water and salt. Bring to boiling. Cover. Reduce heat, and cook slowly until tender, about 30 minutes, depending on size of beets. Drain, reserving liquid in a large bowl.
2. Peel and chop beets, mince the greens.
3. Add beets and greens to reserved liquid along with cucumber, radish, green onion, lemon juice, sour cream, pickle (if desired), and dill. Season with salt and pepper to taste; mix. Chill.
4. Serve garnished with lemon slices and hard-cooked egg and, if desired, whole shrimp.

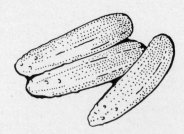

Avocado Yogurt Soup

4 TO 6
SERVINGS

1 cup avocado pulp (2 to 3 avocados, depending on size)
⅔ cup unsweetened yogurt
⅔ cup beef stock, or bouillon made with ⅔ cup water and 1 bouillon cube, then chilled
1 tablespoon lemon juice
1 teaspoon onion juice or grated onion
½ teaspoon salt
Dash Tabasco

1. Put avocado pulp and yogurt into an electric blender and blend until evenly mixed. Adding gradually, blend in beef stock, lemon juice, onion juice, salt, and Tabasco. Chill well.
2. Serve soup in chilled bowls.

Gazpacho

8 TO 10
SERVINGS

1 clove garlic
2 cups chopped peeled fresh tomatoes
1 large cucumber, pared and chopped
½ cup diced green pepper
½ cup chopped onion
1 cup tomato juice
3 tablespoons olive oil
2 tablespoons vinegar
Salt and pepper
Dash Tabasco
½ cup crisp croutons

1. Cut garlic in half and rub onto bottom and sides of a large bowl. Add tomatoes, cucumber, green pepper, onion, tomato juice, olive oil, and vinegar to bowl and stir until evenly mixed. Season to taste with salt, pepper, and Tabasco.
2. Chill in refrigerator at least 1 hour before serving.
3. Serve soup in chilled bowls. Top each serving with a few croutons.

Gazpacho Garden Soup

6 SERVINGS

3 large tomatoes, chopped
1 clove garlic, crushed
1 small cucumber, chopped
1 green pepper, chopped
½ cup sliced green onions
¼ cup chopped onion
¼ cup minced parsley
1 teaspoon crushed rosemary
¼ teaspoon crushed basil
½ teaspoon salt
¼ cup olive oil
¼ cup salad oil
2 tablespoons lemon juice
2 cups chicken broth or 3 chicken bouillon cubes dissolved in 2 cups boiling water, then cooled

1. Combine all ingredients except chicken broth in a large bowl. Toss gently.
2. Stir in chicken broth; chill.
3. Serve in chilled bowls with garnishes suggested in Gazpacho (see page 55).

Crimson Soup

6 SERVINGS

4 cups puréed drained
  tomatoes (about 2
  pounds ripe tomatoes)
1 tablespoon brown sugar
1 teaspoon salt
Few grains freshly
  ground black pepper
½ teaspoon grated lemon
  peel
2 tablespoons lemon juice
½ teaspoon grated onion
1 cup finely chopped
  cantaloupe
½ cup finely chopped
  honeydew melon
¼ cup finely chopped
  cucumber

1. Combine tomato purée, brown sugar, salt, pepper, lemon peel and juice, and onion. Stir in remaining ingredients.
2. Chill several hours.
3. Serve in chilled bowls. If desired, garnish each serving with a lemon slice and a sprig of parsley or watercress. Accompany with a shaker of seasoned salt and a bowl of brown sugar.

Swedish Fruit Soup

12 TO 16
SERVINGS

1 cup dried apricots
¾ cup dried apples
½ cup dried peaches
½ cup prunes
½ cup dark seedless raisins
2 quarts water
¼ cup sugar
3 tablespoons quick-cooking
  tapioca
1 piece stick cinnamon (3
  inches)
1 teaspoon grated orange
  peel
1 cup red raspberry fruit
  syrup

1. Rinse dried fruits with cold water; remove pits from prunes. Place fruits in a large kettle with the water; cover and allow to soak 2 to 3 hours.
2. Add the sugar, tapioca, cinnamon, and orange peel to fruits; let stand 5 minutes. Bring to boiling and simmer covered 1 hour, or until fruit is tender.
3. Stir in syrup; cook, then chill thoroughly.
4. Serve with **whipped cream** and **slivered blanched almonds**.

Norwegian Fruit Soup

ABOUT
3½ CUPS

1 quart water
2 tablespoons rice
½ cup finely chopped apple
1 cup pitted dark sweet
  cherries and juice
½ cup red raspberry fruit
  syrup
¼ cup lemon juice
2-inch piece stick cinnamon
1 tablespoon cold water
1 teaspoon cornstarch

1. Bring 1 quart water to boiling in a deep saucepan.
2. Add 2 tablespoons rice to water so boiling will not stop. Boil rapidly, uncovered, 15 to 20 minutes, or until a kernel is entirely soft when pressed between fingers. Drain rice, reserving liquid.
3. Rinse and finely chop enough apple to yield ½ cup.
4. Put cherries into a bowl.
5. Add fruit syrup and lemon juice.
6. Return the rice water to the saucepan. Add the apple and cinnamon stick.
7. Cook over medium heat 4 to 5 minutes, or until apple is tender. Add the drained rice and the cherry mixture. Remove the cinnamon. Simmer 5 minutes.
8. Blend together cold water and cornstarch to form a smooth paste.
9. Blend cornstarch mixture into soup. Bring to boiling. Continue to cook 3 to 5 minutes. Cool soup slightly.

10. Serve soup warm or cold. If serving soup cold, garnish with **whipped cream.**

Raisin Fruit Soup: Follow recipe for Norwegian Fruit Soup. Omit cherries. Increase red raspberry syrup to 1 cup. Add to the syrup mixture 1 cup (about 5 ounces) dark seedless **raisins.**

Sour Cream Cherry Soup

8 TO 10
SERVINGS

1 quart water
2 to 2½ pounds frozen sweetened tart red cherries, slightly thawed
½ teaspoon salt
½ cup cold water
¼ cup flour
3 egg yolks, slightly beaten
1 cup dairy sour cream

1. Bring the water to boiling in a large saucepan. Add cherries and salt; bring to boiling; simmer, covered, 10 minutes.
2. Pour the cold water into a 1-pint screw-top jar. Add flour; cover jar tightly; shake until blended.
3. Stirring constantly, slowly pour flour mixture into hot cherry mixture; bring to boiling, and cook 2 to 3 minutes.
4. Remove from heat; gradually add ⅓ cup hot soup to the egg yolks, stirring vigorously; blend into soup. Stirring constantly, cook over low heat 3 to 5 minutes (do not boil). Remove from heat.
5. Gradually add 1 cup hot soup to the sour cream, stirring vigorously; then blend into remaining soup. Chill and serve cold.

Cherry Breakfast Soup

6 SERVINGS

1 can (about 10 ounces) dark sweet cherries, drained; reserve liquid
4 whole cloves
1 stick cinnamon, broken in half
Juice of ½ lemon (about 2 tablespoons)
2 teaspoons cornstarch
1 can (16 ounces) sliced pears, drained; reserve juice
1 orange, peeled and sectioned

1. Combine cherry liquid, cloves, cinnamon, and lemon juice in a saucepan; bring to boiling. Simmer 5 minutes. Remove spices with slotted spoon.
2. Combine cornstarch and pear juice; gradually add to cherry mixture. Cook until thickened, stirring constantly.
3. Stir in remaining fruit.

Apricot-Melon Soup

4 SERVINGS

2 cups chopped melon, cantaloupe, or honeydew
2 cups apricot nectar
2 tablespoons lemon juice
Dash salt
1 pint lemon sherbet

1. Combine melon, apricot nectar, lemon juice, and salt. Chill.
2. Serve in chilled bowls. Float a scoop of sherbet on each serving.

SHORT-CUT AND BUDGET SOUPS

Consommé

6 SERVINGS

½ cup coarsely chopped
celery leaves
½ cup chopped leek (green
part only)
½ cup chopped carrots
¼ cup chopped parsley
leaves and stems
2 tomatoes, chopped
3 egg whites
3 egg shells, crushed
2 quarts beef stock

1. Combine ingredients in a heavy 4- or 5-quart saucepot. Bring to boiling. Reduce heat; simmer 20 minutes, uncovered and undisturbed.
2. Pour soup into a sieve lined with a double thickness of dampened cheesecloth which has been placed over a large bowl. Serve hot.

Double Consommé: Follow recipe for Consommé, adding **1 pound beef,** cut in pieces, with vegetables. Simmer 45 minutes.

Consommé with Vegetables: Follow recipe for Consommé. After straining, add **1 cup thinly sliced cooked vegetables.** Heat.

Spicy Tomato Bouillon

ABOUT
6 SERVINGS

1 can (18 ounces) tomato
juice
¼ cup chopped onion
1 tablespoon mixed pickling
spices
1 can (10½ ounces)
condensed beef consommé
¼ teaspoon curry powder
½ cup heavy cream,
whipped

1. Heat together tomato juice, onion, and pickling spices; simmer, uncovered, 20 minutes; strain.
2. Combine tomato mixture with consommé; heat thoroughly.
3. Beat curry powder into whipped cream with final few strokes of beating.
4. To serve, pour tomato-consommé into bowls and top with curry whipped cream.

Caraway Bouillon

6 TO 8
SERVINGS

1½ quarts boiling water
6 beef bouillon cubes
1 tablespoon crushed
caraway seed

1. Add water to bouillon and caraway seed in a saucepan. Stir until cubes are dissolved. Cover; simmer 10 minutes.
2. Serve hot in mugs.

Vegetable Bouillon

4 SERVINGS

1 can (about 10 ounces)
condensed beef broth
1 soup can water
1 can (6 ounces) cocktail
vegetable juice
2 tablespoons finely
chopped green pepper
3 radishes, finely chopped
½ teaspoon instant minced
onion

1. Bring broth, water, and vegetable juice to boiling in a saucepan.
2. Add green pepper, radishes, and onion. Simmer, uncovered, 5 to 8 minutes.
3. Serve hot, garnished with sprigs of **parsley.**

Mixed Vegetables Soup

4 SERVINGS

3 cups beef broth or 3 beef
bouillon cubes dissolved in
3 cups boiling water
1 small potato, diced
2 carrots, diced
1 tomato, chopped
1 green onion, sliced
½ cup shredded cabbage or
½ cup sliced zucchini
½ teaspoon Beau Monde
seasoning or seasoned salt
1 tablespoon minced parsley

1. Combine broth, potato, and carrot in a saucepan; bring to boiling. Simmer 30 minutes.
2. Add remaining ingredients; cook 5 minutes, or until cabbage is crisp-tender.

Egg Drop Soup

3 OR 4 SERVINGS

¼ cup thinly sliced celery
2 tablespoons thinly sliced
mushrooms
1 green onion, thinly sliced
3 cups chicken stock
½ teaspoon salt
Few grains pepper
1 egg, well beaten

1. Combine vegetables and chicken stock in a saucepan. Stir in salt and pepper. Bring to boiling; simmer 5 minutes.
2. Reduce heat and drizzle egg slowly into stock while stirring. Stir until egg separates into shreds. Simmer 1 minute. Serve at once.

Gazpacho

4 SERVINGS

2 cans (6 ounces each)
seasoned tomato juice
½ cucumber, coarsely sliced
1 tomato, quartered
¼ cup vinegar
¼ cup salad oil
1 tablespoon sugar
½ cucumber, chopped
1 tomato, chopped
1 small onion, chopped
Minced parsley
Chopped hard-cooked egg
Chopped cucumber
Croutons

1. Pour the 12 ounces tomato juice into an electric blender. Add sliced cucumber, tomato, vinegar, oil, and sugar; blend.
2. Serve with bowls of parsley, hard-cooked egg, cucumber, and croutons.

Herbed Soup

6 SERVINGS

1 can (about 10 ounces)
condensed chicken
gumbo soup
1 can (about 10 ounces)
condensed cream of
celery soup
2 soup cans water
¼ teaspoon ground fennel
¼ teaspoon crushed basil
Few grains ground ginger
Avocado Sauce

1. Blend soups, water, herbs, and ginger in a saucepan. Simmer covered about 10 minutes.
2. Serve with Avocado Sauce.

Avocado Sauce: Combine ½ cup dairy sour cream and ½ cup mashed ripe avocado; blend until smooth.

Herbed Zucchini Soup

4 TO 6
SERVINGS

½ cup chopped onion
2 tablespoons bacon fat or margarine
4 medium zucchini, sliced (about 4 cups)
1 can (about 10 ounces) condensed beef consommé or broth
2 cups water
1 teaspoon basil
½ teaspoon salt
¼ teaspoon garlic powder
⅛ teaspoon pepper
¼ cup minced parsley or 2 tablespoons dried parsley
Grated Parmesan cheese

1. Sauté onion in bacon fat in a large saucepan. Stir in remaining ingredients except Parmesan cheese. Heat to boiling; simmer until zucchini is tender, 3 to 5 minutes.
2. Sprinkle each serving with Parmesan cheese.

Creamy Zucchini Soup without Cream: Prepare Herbed Zucchini Soup. Purée in an electric blender. Reheat.

Vegetarian Chowder

6 TO 8
SERVINGS

4 cups sliced zucchini
½ cup chopped onion
⅓ cup butter or margarine
⅓ cup flour
2 tablespoons minced parsley
1 teaspoon crushed basil
1 teaspoon salt
⅛ teaspoon pepper
3 cups water
1 chicken bouillon cube
1 package (10 ounces) evaporated milk
1 can (16 ounces) tomatoes, broken up, or 3 tomatoes, skinned and chopped
1 cup shredded Monterey Jack cheese (optional)

1. Sauté zucchini and onion in butter in a large saucepan. Stir in flour, parsley, basil, salt, and pepper.
2. Gradually add water, stirring constantly. Add remaining ingredients. Bring to boiling; simmer 10 to 15 minutes.
3. If desired, stir in Monterey Jack cheese.

Quick Canned Soup with a Zest

2 SERVINGS

1 can (10½ ounces) condensed meat and vegetable soup, any flavor
⅔ cup beer
⅔ cup water

Combine ingredients in a saucepan; heat to simmering. Simmer 2 to 3 minutes.

Vegetable-Sausage Soup

3 SERVINGS

1 can (about 10 ounces) condensed vegetable soup
1 soup can water
½ teaspoon prepared mustard
⅛ teaspoon pepper
1 cup cubed thuringer or cervelat sausage

1. Combine soup, water, mustard, and pepper in a saucepan. Set over moderate heat until mixture begins to simmer.
2. Add the sausage and simmer 10 minutes.

Tomato-Noodle Soup

ABOUT
3½ QUARTS

2 cans (about 10 ounces each) condensed tomato soup
2 cans (about 10 ounces each) condensed cream of celery soup
1 can (6 ounces) tomato paste
¼ cup instant minced onion
1 can (1 ounce) dried instant mixed vegetables
1 teaspoon salt
¼ teaspoon pepper
1 teaspoon crushed basil
2 quarts water
8 ounces (about 4 cups) fine egg noodles
Milk

1. Combine soups and tomato paste in a large saucepan; mix in instant minced onion, instant vegetables, salt, pepper, and basil.
2. Gradually add water, stirring constantly. Bring to boiling, stirring occasionally.
3. Add noodles gradually so the mixture continues to boil. Cook, uncovered, until noodles are tender, about 10 minutes, stirring occasionally. Blend in milk to taste.

Corn Soup

6 TO 8
SERVINGS

½ cup finely chopped onion
2 tablespoons butter
1 quart beef stock or canned beef broth
2½ cups cooked whole kernel golden corn
3 tomatoes, peeled, halved, and seeded
Salt and pepper
1 cup whipping cream
Sour cream

1. Melt butter in a large saucepan. Add onion and cook until soft. Add corn, tomato sauce, and stock. Bring to boiling, reduce heat, and simmer about 10 minutes to blend flavors, stirring frequently.
2. Remove from heat and stir in cream. Season to taste with salt and pepper. Serve hot.

Cream of Everything Soup

ABOUT
8 SERVINGS

1 can (about 10 ounces) condensed cream of mushroom soup
1 can (about 11 ounces) condensed green pea soup
1 can (about 10 ounces) condensed tomato-rice soup
3 soup cans water
½ teaspoon crushed dill weed
¼ teaspoon crushed tarragon
Dairy sour cream

1. Combine all ingredients in a saucepan. Cover and simmer about 10 minutes.
2. Top individual bowls of soup with a dollop of dairy sour cream.

Jiffy Lobster Bisque

5 SERVINGS

1 6½-oz. can lobster meat (about 1 cup, drained)
1½ cups milk
1¼ cups (10½- to 11-oz. can) condensed cream of mushroom soup
1¼ cups (10½- to 11-oz. can) condensed tomato soup
1 teaspoon Worcestershire sauce
5 drops Tabasco
Few grains cayenne pepper
1 tablespoon sherry extract

1. Set out a 2-qt. saucepan.
2. Drain canned lobster meat and break into small pieces.
3. Set lobster aside.
4. Combine milk and mushroom in the saucepan over medium heat.
5. Blend in tomato soup, Worcestershire sauce, Tabasco, and cayenne pepper.
6. Add lobster and bring mixture to boiling.
7. Remove from heat and stir in sherry extract.
8. Serve at once.

Easy Beer-Cheese Soup

7 CUPS;
ABOUT
8 SERVINGS

2 cans (10½ ounces each) condensed cream soup, such as celery, mushroom, or chicken
1 teaspoon Worcestershire sauce
¼ teaspoon seasoned salt
¼ teaspoon paprika
2 cans or bottles (12 ounces each) beer
2 cups shredded Cheddar cheese (8 ounces)
Garnish (optional)

1. In a saucepan, mix soup and seasonings. Add beer gradually while stirring. Heat to simmering.
2. Add cheese. Heat slowly, stirring constantly, until cheese is melted.
3. Pour into soup bowls or cups. Garnish as desired with **croutons, bacon bits, minced parsley,** or **chives.**

Picnic Green Pea Soup

Picnic Green Pea Soup

2 tablespoons chopped onion
¼ cup sliced celery
1 tablespoon butter or margarine
1 can (11¼ ounces) condensed green pea soup
1 soup-can water
1 can (8 ounces) tomatoes, drained and chopped
Thyme croutons

1. Cook onion and celery in butter until tender. Blend in soup; gradually add water, stirring constantly. Add tomatoes and heat, stirring occasionally.
2. Garnish with croutons.
ABOUT 3 SERVINGS

Thyme Croutons: Cut **1 slice white bread** into cubes. Heat 2 tablespoons **butter or margarine** in a skillet; add bread cubes and brown them, stirring constantly. Add a dash of **ground thyme.**

Green Pea Potage

3 SERVINGS

¼ cup dairy sour cream
1 can (about 11 ounces)
 condensed green pea
 soup
1 soup can water
¼ cup sliced water chestnuts
1 tablespoon sliced green
 onion
1 tablespoon lemon juice
Toasted slivered almonds

1. Blend sour cream into soup in a bowl. Gradually add water, stirring until smooth. Mix in water chestnuts, green onion, and lemon juice. Chill 4 hours.
2. Garnish chilled soup with the almonds.

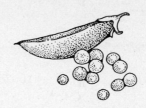

Blender Pea Soup

4 SERVINGS

1 pkg. (10 oz.) frozen peas
2 cups milk
1 tablespoon all-purpose
 flour
2 tablespoons butter or
 margarine
½ teaspoon salt
½ teaspoon nutmeg
⅛ teaspoon pepper
1 small onion, quartered
Chopped parsley

1. Set out a 1½-qt. saucepan.
2. (Cover electric blender container before operating to avoid splashing.)
3. Break apart frozen peas with a fork and set aside.
4. Set out milk.
5. Put into blender container in order, 1 cup of the milk and flour, butter or margarine, salt, nutmeg, pepper and onion.
6. Cover, turn on motor and blend. Continue to blend while gradually adding one-half of peas. Use rubber spatula to scrape down sides of container so that ingredients will become evenly mixed. Blend until contents of container are thoroughly mixed, about 1 to 1½ min. Empty contents of container into saucepan.
7. Pour second cup of milk into container. Blend while gradually adding remaining peas. Stir contents of container into mixture in saucepan. Bring to boiling, stirring occasionally.
8. Serve immediately, topped with parsley.

Main Dish Soup: Follow recipe for Blender Pea Soup. Increase milk to 2½ cups; divide equally for two additions. Gradually add 1 cup cubed, cooked **ham** with last addition of peas. Sliced **frankfurters** added just before heating, may be substituted for ham.

Blender Almond Soup

5 OR 6
SERVINGS

1 cup water
1 cup salted blanched
 almonds
4 egg yolks
3 chicken bouillon cubes
½ slice onion
½ teaspoon sugar
½ teaspoon monosodium
 glutamate
2 cups water
1 cup cream

1. Put all ingredients except 2 cups water and cream into an electric blender container and blend until almonds are finely ground.
2. Pour into a saucepan and stir in the 2 cups water. Cook over low heat 10 to 15 minutes, or until thickened, stirring constantly (do not boil).
3. Stir in the cream and heat thoroughly without boiling. Serve immediately. Garnish with **finely shredded orange peel.**

Snacks

Longing for a snack, the Earl of Sandwich had only hunger and speedy service in mind when he called for his meat to be placed between two slices of bread. Little did he know what he started. In exploring his beguiling creation, homemakers have found that practically every food on earth is in some form or other suitable and indeed delectable as a sandwich filling.

Avocado Sandwiches on Sour Dough

8 SERVINGS

2 avocados, thinly sliced and salted
¼ cup butter (½ stick), softened
½ teaspoon oregano leaves
¼ teaspoon each chervil, parsley flakes, and grated lemon peel
Dash onion powder
8 slices sour dough or Italian bread, diagonally cut

1. Prepare avocado slices.
2. Cream butter with seasonings. Spread thinly over bread.
3. Top with avocado slices. Serve with white wine.

Chicken-Mushroom Sandwiches

SERVES 6

1 cup minced cooked chicken
½ cup (4-oz. can) mushrooms, chopped
¼ cup salted almonds, chopped
3 tablespoons salad dressing
2 tablespoons chopped green olives
¼ teaspoon salt
⅛ teaspoon paprika
6 frankfurter buns, cut in halves

1. Combine the filling ingredients and blend well.
2. Spread between halves of buns.

Cream Cheese Cone Sandwiches

SERVES 9

9 slices bread
3 tablespoons butter, softened
1 pkg. (8 oz.) cream cheese
2 teaspoons cherry jelly
Red food coloring
2 teaspoons orange marmalade
Yellow food coloring
1 teaspoon water
Green food coloring

1. Spread bread slices with butter; trim off crusts.
2. Roll to form cones and fasten with wooden picks.
3. Place on baking sheet and toast in 400°F. oven about 10 minutes.
4. Remove wooden picks.
5. Divide cream cheese into 3 parts.
6. To one part, add cherry jelly and red coloring to give a light pink shade.
7. To second part, add marmalade and enough yellow coloring to give an orange-yellow shade.
8. To third part, add water and green coloring.
9. Using a pastry tube, swirl each color into 3 of the cones.

Avocado Sandwiches on Sour Dough

Glamorous Triple Decker Sandwich

1 SANDWICH

3 slices French toast (see
  Cheese French Toast
  recipe, page 65; omit
  cheese)
1 slice Swiss cheese
1 slice cooked ham
½ teaspoon dry mustard
1 teaspoon water
Sliced cooked chicken

1. Prepare French toast.
2. **To Assemble Sandwich**—Place on top of one slice French toast 1 slice Swiss cheese and 1 slice cooked ham.
3. Top with second French toast slice.
4. Spread with a mixture of dry mustard and water.
5. Place chicken on Mustard mixture.
6. Top with remaining French toast slice.

Yule Sandwich Log

Prepare sandwich fillings: – Deviled ham – peanut butter; egg-bacon; avocado-pineapple; and cheese-shrimp. Prepare cranberry-cheese frosting. Remove crusts from unsliced sandwich loaf and cut lengthwise into 5 slices. Butter 4 slices of bread and spread each with one of the 4 fillings, reserving the cranberry-cheese mixture for top and sides of loaf. Stack the 4 slices and top with the remaining slice of bread. Press loaf firmly together and wrap in plastic wrap. Chill in refrigerator 1 hour. Frost loaf with cranberry-cheese mixture, making lengthwise ridges with a spatula. Garnish platter with cinnamon pear halves placed on lettuce leaves, using maraschino cherries for "bell clappers."

Deviled Ham – Peanut Butter Filling: Combine ⅓ cup peanut butter with 1 can (3 oz.) deviled ham, ¼ cup salad dressing and 3 tablespoons chopped dill pickle.
MAKES ¾ CUP

Egg-Bacon Filling: Combine 2 hard-cooked eggs, chopped, ⅓ cup crumbled cooked bacon and 3 tablespoons salad dressing.
MAKES ¾ CUP

Avocado-Pineapple Filling: Combine ⅓ cup mashed avocado, 2 tablespoons drained, crushed pineapple, 1 teaspoon lemon juice, 1 tablespoon salad dressing and dash salt.
MAKES ½ CUP

Cheese-Shrimp Filling: Combine ½ cup pimiento cream cheese, ½ teaspoon chili sauce, ⅓ cup finely chopped shrimp and ½ teaspoon lemon juice.
MAKES ⅔ CUP

Cranberry-Cheese Frosting: Combine 3 packages (3 oz. each) cream cheese and ⅓ cup strained cranberry sauce. Beat with electric beater until smooth and fluffy.
MAKES 1¾ CUP

Hawaiian Sandwiches

SERVES 6

1 cup minced, cooked
 chicken
½ cup moist, shredded
 coconut
¼ cup salad dressing
2 tablespoons finely chopped
 celery
½ teaspoon lemon juice
½ teaspoon salt
6 frankfurter buns, cut in
 halves

1. Combine the filling ingredients and blend well.
2. Spread between halves of buns.

Taste-Teaser Tuna Sandwiches

4 SANDWICHES

1 cup (7-oz. can, drained)
 flaked tuna
8 slices crisp panbroiled
 bacon, crumbled
¼ cup chopped celery
2 tablespoons chopped
 chives
2 tablespoons chopped
 green pepper
3 tablespoons mayonnaise
⅛ teaspoon freshly ground
 pepper
8 slices white or whole
 wheat bread
Prepared mustard
Process cheese spread
 with pimiento
3 eggs, well beaten
1½ cups milk
¾ teaspoon salt
Sprigs of parsley
Sprinkling of paprika

1. **For Tuna Filling (About 2 cups filling)**—Mix tuna, bacon, celery, chives, green pepper, mayonnaise, and ground pepper thoroughly and set aside.
2. **For Sandwiches**—Lightly grease an 8x8x2-in. baking dish.
3. Arrange bread in two stacks on a flat working surface.
4. With a sharp knife, trim crusts from slices. Spread one side of each slice with prepared mustard.
5. Spread four slices of bread, mustard side up, with the Tuna Filling. Place in baking dish. Top filling with remaining bread slices, placing them mustard side down.
6. Spread Process cheese spread with pimiento lavishly over each sandwich.
7. Set aside.
8. Blend eggs, milk, and salt thoroughly.
9. Pour the egg mixture over the sandwiches.
10. Bake at 325°F 40 min., or until golden brown.
11. Serve sandwiches hot, garnished with parsley and paprika.
12. Accompany with relishes such as **carrot curls** and **radish fans.**

Hearty Sandwich Squares

4 SERVINGS

2 cups pancake mix
1 can (11 ounces) condensed
 Cheddar cheese soup
1 teaspoon prepared mustard
1¼ cups milk
8 slices (1 ounce each) lun-
 cheon meat
4 slices (1 ounce each)
 American cheese
¼ cup chopped onion
¼ cup chopped green pepper

1. Combine pancake, mix, ¼ cup soup, mustard, and 1 cup milk.
2. Spread half the batter in a greased 8-inch square baking dish. Top with meat, cheese, onion, and green pepper. Spoon remaining batter over all.
3. Bake, uncovered, at 400°F 25 to 30 minutes, or until done. Cut into squares to serve. Heat together remaining soup and ¼ cup milk. Spoon over squares. Sprinkle with **snipped parsley.**

Chili Dogs

12 CHILI DOGS

1 pound ground beef
1 tablespoon chili seasoning mix
1 can (15 ounces) tomato sauce with tomato bits
Water
12 skinless frankfurters
12 frankfurter buns

1. Brown ground beef in a skillet; drain. Add seasoning mix and tomato sauce; simmer until flavors are blended.
2. Meanwhile, bring water to boiling in a large saucepan. Add frankfurters, cover, remove from heat, and let stand 7 minutes.
3. Place frankfurters in buns; top with chili mixture.

Cheese-Stuffed Franks in Buns

6 SERVINGS

12 frankfurters
½ cup sweet pickle relish
1 tablespoon prepared mustard
¾ lb. process Cheddar cheese
12 slices bacon
12 buns, buttered and toasted

1. Slit frankfurters almost through lengthwise.
2. Mix together pickle relish and prepared mustard.
3. Cut Cheddar cheese into 12 4x½x½-in. strips.
4. Put one strip of cheese and about 2 teaspoons of the relish mixture into each frankfurter and set aside.
5. Panbroil bacon until partially cooked.
6. Drain. Starting at one end, wrap one slice of bacon around each frankfurter; secure each end with a wooden pick.
7. Set temperature control of range at Broil (500°F or higher). Arrange the bacon-wrapped frankfurters on the broiler rack with tops 3 in. below source of heat and broil until bacon is cooked, turning once.
8. Serve in buns.

French Toast-Cheese Sandwiches

4 SANDWICHES

2 eggs
⅓ cup milk or cream
½ teaspoon salt
8 slices white bread
Prepared mustard
4 slices Swiss or Cheddar cheese
3 tablespoons butter or margarine

1. Set out a heavy skillet.
2. Beat eggs slightly in a shallow bowl.
3. Stir in milk or cream and salt and set aside.
4. Set out bread on a flat working surface.
5. Spread one side of each slice lightly with mustard.
6. Put Swiss or Cheddar cheese on four of the bread slices.
7. Top cheese with remaining bread slices, buttered side down.
8. Heat butter or margarine in the skillet.

9. Dip each sandwich carefully into the egg mixture, coating both sides. Allow excess egg mixture to drain back into bowl. Dip only as many sandwiches at one time as will lie flat in skillet. Cook over low heat until browned. Turn and brown other side.

10. Repeat for remaining sandwiches. If necessary, add more butter or margarine to skillet to prevent sticking.

11. Or place sandwiches on a well-greased baking sheet and brown in oven at 450°F 8 to 10 min.

12. Serve at once.

Cheese French Toast: Follow recipe for French Toast-Cheese Sandwiches. Shred 4 oz. **Swiss cheese** or **Cheddar** (about 1 cup, shredded). Add cheese to egg mixture, beating well. Omit mustard and Swiss cheese slices. Spread slices with egg-cheese mixture and fry.

A Hearty Snack

1 lb. Virginia ham
⅓ cup peas
2 eggs, chopped
4 soft rolls
½ cup mayonnaise
1 tbsp. dill

1. Cut Virginia ham in slices and divide on rolls.
2. Add peas and chopped egg.
3. Top with mayonnaise mixed with dill.

Savory Cheese Sandwiches

6 OPEN-FACE
SANDWICHES

8 oz. Cheddar cheese
(about 2 cups,
shredded)
1 egg
2 tablespoons butter
1 tablespoon chopped onion
1 tablespoon all-purpose
flour
½ cup cream
¼ teaspoon salt
2 drops Tabasco
2 tablespoons lemon juice
1 tablespoon chopped
pimiento
1 tablespoon chopped
stuffed olives
12 slices bacon
6 slices bread
Butter, softened

1. Shred Cheddar cheese and set aside.
2. Hard-cook egg, chop and set aside.
3. Melt butter in a skillet over low heat.
4. Add and cook onion until transparent.
5. Add and stir flour until blended.
6. Heat until mixture bubbles. Remove from heat.
7. Add cream, salt, and Tabasco gradually while stirring constantly.
8. Cook until mixture boils. Cook 1 to 2 min. longer. Remove from heat. Blend in lemon juice.
9. Add to the cream mixture the cheese, egg, pimiento, and stuffed olives.
10. Mix well and set aside.
11. Panbroil bacon until partially cooked.
12. Spread bread with softened butter.
13. Spread cheese mixture on the bread, allowing ¼ cup for each slice. Top each with 2 of the bacon slices, crossed diagonally.
14. Set temperature control of range at Broil (500°F or higher). Arrange sandwiches on broiler rack and place in broiler with tops of sandwiches 3 in. below source of heat. Broil until cheese mixture is bubbly and slightly browned and bacon slices are crisp.
15. Serve hot.

Beer Drinker's Deep-Pan Pizza

ONE LARGE OR
2 SMALL PIZZAS;
4 SERVINGS

Crust:
1 cup warm beer (110° to
120°F)
4 tablespoons olive or salad
oil
1 tablespoon sugar
1½ teaspoons salt
1 package active dry yeast
2¾ to 3¼ cups all-purpose
flour
2 tablespoons cornmeal

Topping:
10 to 12 ounces mozzarella
cheese, shredded or thinly
sliced
1 can (6 ounces) tomato
paste
½ cup beer
2 teaspoons oregano
1 teaspoon fennel seed
(optional)
½ teaspoon sugar
¾ to 1 pound bulk pork or
Italian sausage, broken up
½ cup grated Parmesan
cheese

1. For crust, combine in a large bowl the warm beer, 2 tablespoons oil, sugar, salt, and yeast. Add 1½ cups flour; beat until smooth. Stir in enough additional flour to make a fairly stiff dough.
2. Turn dough out onto a lightly floured surface. Knead until smooth and elastic (about 5 minutes). Place dough in a greased bowl, turning once to grease top. Cover and let rise in warm place (85°F) until double in bulk (about 1 hour).
3. Punch dough down. (For 2 small pizzas, divide in half.) Using 2 tablespoons oil, coat a 14-inch round deep pizza pan. (Or use two 9-inch round cake pans.) Sprinkle with cornmeal. Pat dough into pan, pinching up a rim around the edge. Cover and let rise in a warm place until double in bulk (about 30 minutes).
4. For topping, mix tomato paste, beer, oregano, fennel seed, and sugar. Cover pizza dough evenly with mozzarella cheese; evenly spoon on tomato paste mixture. Sprinkle with sausage, then top with Parmesan cheese.
5. Bake at 450°F 15 to 20 minutes, or until crust is browned and sausage is cooked.

Note: Alternate toppings could be (1) **1 can (4 ounces) sliced mushrooms, drained,** or (2) **8 anchovies** plus ⅓ **cup chopped ripe olives,** or (3) ½ **pound sliced pepperoni.** Omit or reduce the sausage, but include cheeses and tomato sauce.

Beer Drinker's Deep-Pan Pizza

Tomato-Cheese Pizza

Tomato-Cheese Pizza

6 TO 8
SERVINGS

½ package active dry yeast
1 cup plus 2 tablespoons
warm water
4 cups sifted all-purpose
flour
1 teaspoon salt
3 cups drained canned
tomatoes
8 ounces mozzarella cheese,
thinly sliced
½ cup olive oil
¼ cup grated Parmesan
cheese
1 teaspoon salt
½ teaspoon pepper
2 teaspoons oregano

1. Soften yeast in 2 tablespoons warm water. Set aside.
2. Pour remaining cup of warm water into a large bowl. Blend in 2 cups flour and 1 teaspoon salt. Stir softened yeast and add to flour-water mixture, mixing well.
3. Add about 1 cup flour to yeast mixture and beat until very smooth. Mix in enough remaining flour to make a soft dough. Turn dough onto a lightly floured surface and allow to rest 5 to 10 minutes. Knead 5 to 8 minutes, until dough is smooth and elastic.
4. Shape dough into a smooth ball and place in a greased bowl just large enough to allow dough to double. Turn dough to bring greased surface to top. Cover with waxed paper and let stand in warm place (about 80°) until dough is doubled (about 1½ to 2 hours).
5. Punch down with fist. Fold edge towards center and turn dough over. Divide dough into two equal balls. Grease another bowl and place one of the balls in it. Turn dough in both bowls so greased side is on top. Cover and let rise again until almost doubled (about 45 minutes).
6. Roll each ball of dough into a 14x10-inch rectangle, ⅛ inch thick. Place on two lightly greased 15½x12-inch baking sheets. Shape edges by pressing dough between thumb and forefinger to make a ridge. If desired, dough may be rolled into rounds, ⅛ inch thick.
7. Force tomatoes through a sieve or food mill and spread 1½ cups on each pizza. Arrange 4 ounces of mozzarella cheese on each pizza. Sprinkle over each pizza, in the order given, ¼ cup olive oil, 2 tablespoons grated Parmesan cheese, ½ teaspoon salt, ¼ teaspoon pepper, and 1 teaspoon oregano.
8. Bake at 400°F 25 to 30 minutes, or until crust is browned. Cut into wedges to serve.

Mushroom Pizza: Follow Tomato-Cheese Pizza recipe. Before baking, place on each pizza 1 cup (8-ounce can) drained **mushroom buttons.**

Sausage Pizza: Follow Tomato-Cheese Pizza recipe. Before baking, place on each pizza 1 pound **hot Italian sausage** (with casing removed), cut in ¼-inch pieces.

Anchovy Pizza: Follow Tomato-Cheese Pizza recipe. Omit mozzarella and Parmesan cheeses, decrease amount of oregano to ¼ teaspoon, and top each pizza with **anchovy fillets,** cut in ¼-inch pieces.

Miniature Pizzas: Follow Tomato-Cheese Pizza recipe. After rolling dough, cut dough into 3½-inch rounds. Shape edge of rounds as in Tomato-Cheese Pizza recipe. Using half the amount of ingredients in that recipe, spread each pizza with 2 tablespoons sieved canned tomatoes. Top with a slice of mozzarella cheese. Sprinkle cheese with ½ teaspoon olive oil, ½ teaspoon grated Parmesan cheese, and

(continued)

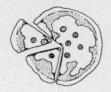

a few grains salt and pepper. Bake at 400°F 15 to 20 minutes, or until crust is browned.
ABOUT 24 MINIATURE PIZZAS

English Muffin Pizzas: Split 12 **English muffins** and spread cut sides with **butter or margarine.** Toast under the broiler until lightly browned. Top each half as for Miniature Pizza. Bake at 400°F 5 to 8 minutes, or until tomato mixture is bubbling hot.
24 PIZZAS

Tuna in a Cucumber

1 can (7 oz.) tuna
1 pkg. (3 oz.) cream cheese
1 tablespoon mayonnaise
1 tablespoon lemon juice
½ teaspoon salt
¼ teaspoon pepper
1 tablespoon pickle relish
3 small cucumbers

1. Thoroughly blend first 7 ingredients together. Chill.
2. Core the cucumbers to remove centers.
3. Stuff tuna mixture into cavities and chill.
4. Slice and serve on assorted crackers.

Stuffed Celery Rings

SERVES 8

1 medium bunch celery
Tangy cheese spread
French dressing

1. Cut the top from bunch celery.
2. Wash and dry each stalk.
3. Fill smallest stalks with cheese spread, then fill next smallest stalks and press firmly against first stalks.
4. Continue filling and pressing stalks together until all the celery is formed into a bunch. Tie firmly with string; chill.
5. Slice crosswise into thin slices and serve on lettuce or watercress. Sprinkle with French dressing.

Note: If desired, use Roquefort spread instead of tangy cheese spread.

Blue Cheese in a Melon

½ pound blue cheese
1 pkg. (8 oz.) cream cheese
¼ cup heavy cream
1 ripe cantaloupe

1. Thoroughly blend the blue and cream cheese together; beat in the cream until fluffy.
2. Using a melon-ball cutter, scoop melon balls from ripe cantaloupe.
3. Spoon cheese dip into cantaloupe shell.
4. Serve with assorted crackers and melon balls on cocktail picks.

Soups and Snacks from the Microwave Oven

What more elegant way to impress your guests than by serving a hot soup as the first course? Soups made in the microwave oven let you cook with an ease that you never dreamed possible. With microwave cooking, you needn't worry about your soups scorching. They need less attention than when cooked conventionally and, best of all, need less stirring. Soups with a milk base boil over quickly, so use a container that is twice the ingredient volume.

A steaming cup of soup makes a tasty and nutritious between-meal snack. It can also dress up an ordinary lunch or stand on its own as a hearty meal. Soup can be made in the microwave oven right in the serving dish; individual servings can be made in bowls or mugs so there is an absolute minimum of cleanup.

Tired of the same old lunch-meat sandwich? With microwave cooking, cold sandwiches can be transformed into piping-hot, tasty treats. The addition of a bowl of soup or salad can create a whole meal. When making sandwiches, follow the same tips as for reheating bread; do not overheat. Place sandwiches on paper towels or a roast rack to prevent the bottom of the bread from getting wet and soggy.

Hot Tuna Canapés (page 74)

New England Clam Chowder

4 TO 6 SERVINGS

2 tablespoons butter
½ cup diced celery
¼ cup minced onion
¼ cup minced green pepper
1¾ cups milk
1 cup cream or
half-and-half
3 tablespoons flour
½ cup diced potato
2 cans (7½ ounces each)
minced clams, drained;
reserve liquid
½ teaspoon salt
⅛ teaspoon thyme
3 drops Tabasco
½ teaspoon Worcestershire
sauce

1. Put butter, celery, onion and green pepper into a 3-quart glass casserole. Cook uncovered in microwave oven 3 minutes at HIGH, or until vegetables are tender; stir after 1 minute. Remove from oven.
2. Combine milk and cream in a glass bowl. Scald uncovered in microwave oven (2½ minutes at HIGH).
3. Blend flour into the vegetable-butter mixture. Add the scalded milk and cream gradually, stirring constantly. Cook uncovered in microwave oven 2½ minutes at HIGH, or until boiling.
4. Stir potato, reserved clam liquid, salt, thyme and Tabasco into sauce. Cook uncovered in microwave oven 3 minutes at HIGH, or until boiling. Stir. Cook uncovered 15 minutes at SIMMER; stir 3 times.
5. Add clams and Worcestershire sauce to mixture in casserole; stir. Cook uncovered in microwave oven to serving temperature (1½ minutes at HIGH).

Manhattan Clam Chowder

4 SERVINGS

4 slices bacon
1 can (8 ounces) minced
clams
2 medium potatoes, pared
and cubed
¼ cup chopped onion
1 can (16 ounces) whole
tomatoes (undrained)
2 tablespoons flour
1 teaspoon salt
¼ teaspoon pepper
½ teaspoon oregano

1. Arrange bacon on the rack in a 2-quart glass baking dish. Cook 2 to 3 minutes, rotating dish one-quarter turn halfway through cooking time. Lift rack from dish; set bacon aside.
2. Drain clams, reserving liquor. Add clam liquor, potatoes, onion, and tomatoes to drippings in dish and cook, covered, 10 to 12 minutes, stirring halfway through cooking time.
3. Blend flour with ¼ cup hot liquid from dish. Stir salt, pepper, oregano, and clams into flour mixture. Add to liquid in dish, blending well. Cook, covered, 5 to 6 minutes or until mixture boils, stirring every 2 minutes.
4. Rest, covered, 5 minutes before serving. Garnish with cooked bacon.

Clam-and-Corn Chowder

4 TO 6 SERVINGS

4 slices bacon, cooked
1 small onion, thinly sliced
1 can (16 ounces) New
England-style clam
chowder
2 cups milk
1 can (12 ounces) corn,
drained
¼ teaspoon thyme
½ teaspoon salt
¼ teaspoon pepper

1. When bacon is cold, crumble in bits; set aside.
2. Sauté onion in bacon drippings 2 to 3 minutes; set aside.
3. In a 2-quart glass casserole, combine clam chowder, milk, corn, and thyme. Stir in onion.
4. Cook 4 to 5 minutes, stirring every minute, until mixture steams. Stir in salt and pepper.
5. Serve garnished with bacon bits.

Vegetable Oyster Soup

ABOUT
7 CUPS

4 cups chopped head lettuce
2 cups chopped spinach
1 cup chopped carrots
½ cup chopped onion
1½ cups chicken broth or 1 can (about 10 ounces) chicken broth
1 can (10 ounces) frozen oysters, thawed
2 tablespoons butter
2 tablespoons flour
1¼ teaspoons salt
2 cups milk
1 teaspoon grated lemon peel
1 tablespoon lemon juice
Freshly ground pepper
Lemon slices

1. Put lettuce, spinach, carrots, onion, ½ cup chicken broth and oysters into a 4-quart glass bowl. Cover with waxed paper. Cook in microwave oven 12 to 14 minutes at HIGH, or until carrots are crisp-tender; stir occasionally.
2. Turn half of mixture into an electric blender container and blend a few seconds; repeat for second half of mixture. Set blended mixture aside.
3. Melt butter in a 1½-quart glass bowl in microwave oven (30 seconds at HIGH).
4. Stir flour and salt into melted butter. Gradually stir in milk and remaining 1 cup chicken broth. Cook uncovered in microwave oven about 10 minutes at HIGH, or until thickened; stir occasionally.
5. Add vegetable mixture, lemon peel and juice and pepper. Heat uncovered in microwave oven to serving temperature (3 to 4 minutes at HIGH).
6. Serve garnished with lemon slices.

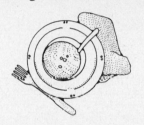

Mock Bouillabaisse

3 OR 4
SERVINGS

1 small onion, sliced
1 clove garlic, minced
1 bay leaf
¼ teaspoon thyme
2 tablespoons olive oil
1 can (10¾ ounces) condensed tomato soup
¾ soup can water
2 cups cooked seafood
1 teaspoon lemon juice
Dash Tabasco
3 or 4 slices French bread, toasted

1. In a 3-quart glass casserole, combine onion, garlic, bay leaf, thyme, and olive oil. Cook 3 to 4 minutes, stirring halfway through cooking time, until onion is tender.
2. Stir in soup, water, seafood, lemon juice, and Tabasco.
3. Heat 6 to 8 minutes, stirring every 2 minutes, until boiling.
4. Cover and cook an additional 2 minutes.
5. Rest 5 minutes. Ladle soup over toast in bowls.

Tomato-Leek Soup

4 SERVINGS

2 tablespoons butter
2 leeks, chopped (about 2½ cups)
2 carrots, finely diced (about 1 cup)
2 tablespoons flour
2 beef bouillon cubes
2 cups boiling water
1 to 2 teaspoons sugar
¼ teaspoon salt
4 large ripe tomatoes (2 pounds), peeled and cut in pieces

1. Heat butter in a 2½-quart glass bowl about 30 seconds. Add leeks and carrots and heat 4 to 5 minutes, stirring halfway through cooking.
2. Stir in flour and heat 1 to 1½ minutes.
3. Dissolve bouillon cubes in water and stir into the vegetables. Bring to boiling, about 2½ to 3 minutes, stirring after every minute. Continue cooking 4 minutes, stirring after 2 minutes.
4. Stir in sugar, salt, and tomatoes. Heat 20 to 25 minutes, stirring every 5 minutes, until tomatoes are soft.

Creamed Onion Soup

8 SERVINGS

4 medium onions, sliced
½ cup butter
¼ cup flour
1 quart milk
2 cups chicken broth or 2 chicken bouillon cubes dissolved in 2 cups boiling water
1 to 1½ teaspoons salt
1 egg yolk
1 tablespoon minced parsley
½ cup croutons

1. In a 3-quart casserole, sauté onions in butter 4 to 5 minutes, stirring every minute. Stir in flour and cook until sauce bubbles, about 1 minute.
2. Add milk slowly, stirring gently. Cook until slightly thickened, about 6 to 8 minutes, stirring every 2 minutes.
3. Add broth and cook 5 minutes, stirring twice.
4. Stir in salt to taste. Blend some of the hot soup with egg yolk and return to remaining soup. Cook 1 minute, stirring every 15 seconds.
5. Serve topped with minced parsley and croutons.

Frankfurter Reuben

6 SERVINGS

12 slices rye bread
Butter
6 large frankfurters
⅓ cup Thousand Island dressing
1 cup sauerkraut, well drained
6 slices Swiss cheese

1. Toast bread, and butter each piece on 1 side. Split frankfurters in half lengthwise and place on buttered side of 6 slices toast. Spread dressing on frankfurters, and top each sandwich with about 2 tablespoons sauerkraut. Top each with slice of remaining bread, buttered side towards cheese.
2. Cook as follows, rotating one-quarter turn halfway through cooking time: 45 to 60 seconds for 1 sandwich; 2 to 2½ minutes for 3 sandwiches; and 3 to 4 minutes for 6 sandwiches.
3. Serve warm.

Hot Tuna Canapés (Pictured on page 71)

1 can (6½ or 7 ounces) tuna
¼ cup mayonnaise
1 tablespoon ketchup
¼ teaspoon salt
Few grains cayenne pepper
2 teaspoons finely chopped onion
¼ teaspoon Worcestershire sauce
1 cucumber
Paprika (optional)
48 Melba toast rounds
12 pimento-stuffed olives, sliced

1. Drain and flake tuna. Add mayonnaise, ketchup, salt, cayenne pepper, onion and Worcestershire sauce.
2. Pare cucumber and slice paper-thin (if desired, sprinkle with paprika).
3. For each canapé, place cucumber slice on toast round, pile tuna mixture in center and top with olive slice.
4. Put 8 canapés in circle on 6 individual paper plates. For each plate, cook uncovered in microwave oven 30 to 60 seconds.

Bacon Cheese-Melt Sandwiches

4 SANDWICHES

6 slices bacon, halved
4 slices bread
Butter
4 large tomato slices
4 pasteurized process American cheese slices

1. Arrange bacon on a roast rack set in a 2-quart glass baking dish. Cover with a paper towel. Cook in microwave oven 5 minutes.
2. Meanwhile, toast bread and lightly spread with butter.
3. Put toast on roast rack and top with bacon pieces. Put a tomato slice on each toast slice, and then a slice of cheese. Heat uncovered in microwave oven 2 minutes, or until cheese melts. Serve immediately.

Bacon Cheese-Melt Sandwiches

Canadian Mushroom Sandwiches

6 OPEN-FACED
SANDWICHES

6 kaiser rolls
Butter or margarine,
softened
1 tablespoon chopped
uncooked bacon
2 tablespoons chopped onion
1 jar (2 ounces) sliced
mushrooms, drained
1 teaspoon snipped parsley
18 slices (about 1 pound)
smoked pork loin Canadian-
style bacon, cut ⅛ inch
thick
6 slices (1 ounce each) Swiss
cheese
6 thin green pepper rings
Paprika

1. Split rolls; if desired, reserve tops to accompany open-faced sandwiches. Spread roll bottoms with butter.
2. Combine bacon, onion, mushrooms and parsley in a 2-cup glass measuring cup. Cook uncovered in microwave oven about 2 minutes, or until onion is tender; stir once.
3. Arrange 3 slices Canadian bacon on each buttered roll and top with mushroom mixture and 1 slice cheese. Place 1 green pepper ring on each cheese slice; sprinkle paprika inside ring.
4. Place sandwiches on paper towels or roast rack. Heat uncovered in microwave oven 4 to 6 minutes, or until cheese is bubbly and meat is hot.
6. Serve sandwiches garnished with a **cherry tomato** and a **pimento-stuffed olive** on each skewer.

Cheese and Bacon Sandwiches

6 SANDWICHES

12 slices wheat bread,
  toasted
6 slices process American
  cheese
12 slices bacon, cooked and
  cut in half
6 slices Swiss cheese

1. On each of 6 toast slices, place 1 slice American cheese, 4 bacon halves, and 1 slice Swiss cheese. Top with remaining pieces of toast.
2. Cook as follows, rotating one-quarter turn halfway through cooking time: 45 to 60 seconds for 1 sandwich; 2 to 2½ minutes for 3 sandwiches; and 3 to 4 minutes for 6 sandwiches.
3. Serve warm.

Tortilla Sandwiches

12 SANDWICHES

12 corn tortillas
Salad oil
6 slices Monterey Jack
  cheese

1. Fry tortillas in small amount of hot oil on range until limp. Fold in half and hold slightly open with tongs; continue to fry until crisp, turning to fry on both sides. Drain on paper towel.
2. Place ½ slice cheese in each tortilla. Arrange tortillas in shallow glass dish in microwave and cook 1 to 1½ minutes, rotating dish one-quarter turn halfway through cooking time.
3. Serve hot; reheat if needed.

Stromboli Sandwich

6 SERVINGS

1 pound ground beef
2 tablespoons finely chopped
  onion
½ cup tomato sauce
½ cup ketchup
2 tablespoons grated
  Parmesan cheese
½ teaspoon garlic salt
¼ teaspoon oregano
½ teaspoon garlic powder
¼ cup butter
6 French rolls
6 slices mozzarella cheese

1. In a 1½-quart glass casserole, combine ground beef and onion. Cook 4 to 5 minutes, stirring halfway through cooking time. Spoon off drippings.
2. Stir in tomato sauce, ketchup, Parmesan cheese, garlic salt, and oregano. Cook, covered, 5 to 6 minutes, stirring halfway through cooking time.
3. In a 1-cup glass measure, combine garlic powder and butter; heat 30 seconds. Stir to blend. Pour melted butter evenly over inside of top half of each roll.
4. Divide meat mixture evenly and spread on bottom halves of each roll. Top with 1 slice mozzarella, place tops on buns, and wrap each in a napkin.
5. Cook as follows, rotating one-quarter turn halfway through cooking time: 30 to 45 seconds for 1 sandwich; 1½ to 2 minutes for 3 sandwiches; and 3 to 4 minutes for 6 sandwiches.
6. Serve warm.

Cheese Rolls

8 CHEESE ROLLS

8 hot dog buns or French
  rolls
Soft butter
½ cup grated Parmesan
  cheese
⅓ cup poppy seed

1. Slice each roll in half lengthwise. Spread all cut sides with soft butter.
2. In a glass pie plate, mix cheese and poppy seed. Press buttered sides of each roll in cheese mixture.
3. Wrap 4 rolls in paper towel, napkin, or terry towel and cook 45 seconds to 1 minute. Repeat procedure with remaining 4 rolls.

Conventional oven: Bake at 350°F 10 to 12 minutes.

Welsh Rabbit

4 SANDWICHES

2 tablespoons butter
2 cups shredded Cheddar
  cheese
1 cup beer
½ teaspoon dry mustard
¼ teaspoon Tabasco
4 slices toast

1. In a 2-quart glass casserole, heat butter 30 seconds. Add cheese and cook 1 to 2 minutes until cheese begins to melt, stirring halfway through cooking time.
2. Stir in beer, mustard, and Tabasco. Heat 1 minute.
3. Serve hot on toast.

Index